INSTANT ANSWERS

for

King's Kids

in Training

by Harold Hill

*Compiled by Gretchen Zimmer Black
with Irene Burk Harrell*

Logos International
Plainfield, New Jersey

Instant Answers for King's Kids in Training
Copyright © 1978 by Logos International
201 Church Street, Plainfield, New Jersey 07060

All Rights Reserved
Printed in the United States of America
Library of Congress Catalog Card Number: 78-58862
International Standard Book Number: 0-88270-277-7

Directions for the Use of the Instant Answer Book

Hi King's Kids!

Here's what you've been waiting for . . . a whole bookful of *Instant Answers* to just about everything that can happen to you today . . . dozens of solutions . . . right at your fingertips.

What's your problem? Is it related to Business . . . Emotions . . . Family . . . Travel . . . Habits . . . Health . . . Money . . . People . . . Religion . . . Drinking Too Much . . . Husband-Wife Haggles . . . ? Or is it simply a Mixed and Matched Bag of other Assorted Woes?

Whatever your problem, you know that God has all the answers. But sometimes, the answers are hard to find. That's where *Instant Answers* comes in.

Instant Answers offers help in a hurry. Instead of rooting through sixty-six Bible books plus a concordance or two, you can simply follow the directions and be quickly on your way rejoicing and praising God for His goodness to His young'uns.

Remember, God is no respecter of persons. What He has done for one, He will do for all. Here's how to find what He has done for you:

1. Find your problem, or one like it, in the *Instant Answer* book. It's all alphabetically arranged, just like the dictionary.
2. Read God's answer to the problem in the Scriptures printed below your problem.
3. While you're meditating on His answer, turn to the relevant King's kid experiences reported in my first four books:

Example:

Under the topic **Drinking Too Much,** you will find a section labeled *King's kid report,* containing the notation, "King's Kid 11-16; Winner 191-93; Victory 1-10, 12-14." This means that the subject of drinking too much is discussed on pages 11-16 of *How to Live Like a King's Kid*, pages 191-93 of *How to Be a Winner*, and pages 1-10 and 12-14 of *How to Live in High Victory*.

4. When you have read the report, make a record of your own experience to share with others in their time of similar need. That's scriptural too! (2 Corinthians 1:3-7).

Simple enough? That's all there is to it, but here are some further hints for best results:

1. Get a really solid handle on the Word of God and refuse to be impressed by appearances. Soak in the truth of Romans 8:28 in *every* situation: "And we KNOW that all things work together for good to them that love God, to them who are the called according to his purpose." (That's talking about real King's kids, all right.)

2. Make certain you have no hidden roadblocks such as unforgiveness, impatience, unbelief, resentments, and their scroungy relatives which are always trying to hinder or block the arrival of answers to prayer.

3. Detach emotionally from ownership of the problem, by praising Jesus the new owner to whom you have transferred title.

4. Do NOT be a clock-watcher (2 Peter 3:9, Hebrews 12:1). Allow God a reasonable amount of time. Remember how long it took you to get into that mess by your own very best efforts!

5. Watch carefully for the answer . . . it may appear in a

totally unexpected manner . . . far better than anything you could have dreamed up yourself.

According to Romans 10:17 in the *Manufacturer's Handbook*, "Faith cometh by hearing, and hearing by the word of God" in action in the lives of other King's kids who have tried it and reported how it works for them.

Drop me a line % Logos International, Plainfield, NJ 07060, and let me know how these *Instant Answers* work for you.

Harold Hill, Reporter
King's Kid in Training

P.S. The *Instant Answer* book is good for something else, too. To quickly locate a particular incident in any one of the first four King's kid books, simply look under a key word in the *Instant Answer* book . . . **Liebman's Glory Meter; Mercedes-Benz; Missing Day,** etc. Happy Hunting!

Other books by Harold Hill:

How to Live Like a King's Kid
How Did It All Begin? (From Goo to You by Way of the Zoo)
How to Be a Winner
How to Live in High Victory

INSTANT
ANSWERS
for
King's Kids
in Training

Accidents. See **Broken Bones; Highway Accidents**
Adam and Eve, Goo 51-56; Victory 40-41, 297
Adversity. See **Praise in Adversity; Troubles**

Air Travel Problems

God's answer: Rejoice evermore. Pray without ceasing. In every thing give thanks: for this is the will of God in Christ Jesus concerning you. (1 Thessalonians 5:16-18)

Yes, be bold and strong! Banish fear and doubt! For remember, the Lord your God is with you wherever you go. (Joshua 1:9 TLB)

And we know that all things work together for good to them that love God, to them who are the called according to his purpose. (Romans 8:28)

Rest in the Lord, and wait patiently for him. (Psalm 37:7a)

King's kid report: King's Kid 1-6, 139-42; Winner 113-15, 151-57

My personal experience:

1

Alanon Family Groups

God's answer: Bear ye one another's burdens, and so fulfil the law of Christ. (Galatians 6:2)

Let us be concerned for one another, to help one another to show love and to do good. Let us not give up the habit of meeting together, as some are doing. Instead, let us encourage one another all the more. . . . (Hebrews 10:24-25 TEV)

Blessed be God, even the Father of our Lord Jesus Christ, the Father of mercies, and the God of all comfort; Who comforteth us in all our tribulation, that we may be able to comfort them which are in any trouble, by the comfort wherewith we ourselves are comforted of God. (2 Corinthians 1:3-4)

King's kid report: Victory 7

My personal experience:

Alcohol. See **Drinking Too Much**

Angels

God's answer: For he shall give his angels charge over thee, to keep thee in all thy ways. (Psalm 91:11)

What are the angels, then? They are spirits who serve God and are sent by him to help those who are to receive salvation. (Hebrews 1:14 TEV)

King's kid report: King's Kid 21-22; Winner 91; Victory 307-12

My personal experience:

Angels of Light

God's answer: And no marvel; for Satan himself is transformed into an angel of light. Therefore it is no great thing if his ministers also be transformed as the ministers of righteousness; whose end shall be according to their works. (2 Corinthians 11:14-15)

King's kid report: Victory 281-92

My personal experience:

4

Anger

God's answer: If you are angry, don't sin by nursing your grudge. Don't let the sun go down with you still angry—get over it quickly; for when you are angry you give a mighty foothold to the devil. (Ephesians 4:26-27 TLB)

The fool who provokes his family to anger and resentment will finally have nothing worthwhile left. (Proverbs 11:29 TLB)

Wherefore, my beloved brethren, let every man be swift to hear, slow to speak, slow to wrath: For the wrath of man worketh not the righteousness of God. (James 1:19-20)

King's kid report: Victory 199; Goo 62

My personal experience:

5

Anti-Mudites

God's answer: Now I beseech you, brethren, mark them which cause divisions and offences contrary to the doctrine which ye have learned; and avoid them. (Romans 16:17)

Now I beseech you, brethren, by the name of our Lord Jesus Christ, that ye all speak the same thing, and that there be no divisions among you; but that ye be perfectly joined together in the same mind and in the same judgment. (1 Corinthians 1:10)

King's kid report: Victory 117

My personal experience:

Anxiety (see also **Stress)**

God's answer: Casting all your care upon him; for he careth for you. (1 Peter 5:7)

And besides, what's the use of worrying? What good does it do? Will it add a single day to your life? Of course not! He will always give you all you need from day to day if you will make the Kingdom of God your primary concern. (Luke 12:25, 31 TLB)

Don't worry about anything; instead, pray about everything; tell God your needs and don't forget to thank him for his answers. (Philippians 4:6 TLB)

King's kid report: Goo 63, 76; Winner 135-41; Victory 107

My personal experience:

7

Armor of God
God's answer: Wherefore take unto you the whole armour of God, that ye may be able to withstand in the evil day, and having done all, to stand. Stand therefore, having your loins girt about with truth, and having on the breastplate of righteousness; And your feet shod with the preparation of the gospel of peace; Above all, taking the shield of faith, wherewith ye shall be able to quench all the fiery darts of the wicked. And take the helmet of salvation, and the sword of the Spirit, which is the word of God. (Ephesians 6:13-17)

My personal experience:

Arthritis

God's answer: Be not wise in thine own eyes: fear the Lord, and depart from evil. It shall be health to thy navel, and marrow to thy bones. (Proverbs 3:7-8)

When I pray, you answer me, and encourage me by giving me the strength I need. (Psalm 138:3 TLB)

Confess your faults one to another, and pray one for another, that ye may be healed. (James 5:16a)

King's kid report: King's Kid 108-11; Goo 77-78; Winner 82-83; Victory 192-94

My personal experience:

9

Atoms

God's answer: For by him were all things created, that are in heaven, and that are in earth, visible and invisible, whether they be thrones, or dominions, or principalities, or powers: all things were created by him, and for him: And he is before all things, and by him all things consist. (Colossians 1:16-17)

King's kid report: Goo 60-61, 80-81

My personal experience:

Attendance, Miserable

God's answer: For where two or three are gathered together in my name, there am I in the midst of them. (Matthew 18:20)

King's kid report: Victory 205-11

My personal experience:

Authority. See **Rebellion**

Automatic Writing
  God's answer: Beloved, believe not every spirit, but try
  the spirits whether they are of God: because many false
  prophets are gone out into the world. Hereby know ye the
  Spirit of God: Every spirit that confesseth that Jesus
  Christ is come in the flesh is of God. (1 John 4:1-2)

  King's kid report: King's Kid 179

  My personal experience:

Backbiting. See **Tongue Trouble**

Back Trouble
God's answer: He sent his word, and healed them, and delivered them from their destructions. (Psalm 107:20)

Beloved, I wish above all things that thou mayest prosper and be in health, even as thy soul prospereth. (3 John 2)

And these signs shall follow them that believe; they shall lay hands on the sick and they shall recover. (Mark 16:17a, 18b)

King's kid report: King's Kid 39-43; Victory 99-103

My personal experience:

Bad debts. See **Debts**
Banquets, Victory 263-64

Baptism in the Holy Spirit (see also **Power Shortage**)
God's answer: Repent, and be baptized every one of you in
the name of Jesus Christ for the remission of sins, and ye
shall receive the gift of the Holy Ghost. (Acts 2:38)

Behold the Lamb of God, which taketh away the sin of the
world . . . the same is he which baptizeth with the Holy
Ghost. (John 1:29b, 33b)

If ye then, being evil, know how to give good gifts unto
your children: how much more shall your heavenly Father
give the Holy Spirit to them that ask him? (Luke 11:13)

(For as yet he was fallen upon none of them: only they
were baptized in the name of the Lord Jesus.) Then laid
they their hands on them, and they received the Holy
Ghost. (Acts 8:16-17)

Have ye received the Holy Ghost since ye believed? (Acts
19:2a)

King's kid report: King's Kid 45-58, 65; Goo 83-86; Winner
15-26, 75-77; Victory 83-89, 250-52

My personal experience:

Baptism, Water

God's answer: For as many of you as have been baptized into Christ have put on Christ. (Galatians 3:27)

Therefore we are buried with him by baptism into death: that like as Christ was raised up from the dead by the glory of the Father, even so we also should walk in newness of life. (Romans 6:4)

And as they went on their way, they came unto a certain water: and the eunuch said, See, here is water; what doth hinder me to be baptized? And Philip said, If thou believest with all thine heart, thou mayest. And he answered and said, I believe that Jesus Christ is the Son of God. (Acts 8:36-37)

He that believeth and is baptized shall be saved. (Mark 16:16a)

In Him also you were circumcised with a circumcision not made with hands, but in a (spiritual) circumcision (performed by) Christ by stripping off the body of the flesh (the whole corrupt, carnal nature with its passions and lusts). (Thus you were circumcised when) you were buried with Him in (your) baptism, in which you were also raised with Him (to a new life) through (your) faith in the

15

working of God (as displayed) when He raised Him up from the dead. (Colossians 2:11-12 TAB)

King's kid report: King's Kid 25, 45-46, 49-51; Goo 66; Victory 164-65

My personal experience:

Bathsheba. See **David and Bathsheba**

Bathtub, Parable of the
God's answer: Let that therefore abide in you, which ye
have heard from the beginning. If that which ye have
heard from the beginning shall remain in you, ye also shall
continue in the Son, and in the Father. (1 John 2:24)

King's kid report: Victory 27-28

My personal experience:

Bedmates

God's answer: Not that I speak in respect of want: for I have learned, in whatsoever state I am, therewith to be content. (Philippians 4:11)

King's kid report: Victory 118-20

My personal experience:

Bias

God's answer: But the man who isn't a Christian can't understand and can't accept these thoughts from God, which the Holy Spirit teaches us. They sound foolish to him, because only those who have the Holy Spirit within them can understand what the Holy Spirit means. Others just can't take it in. But the spiritual man has insight into everything, and that bothers and baffles the man of the world, who can't understand him at all. How could he? For certainly he has never been one to know the Lord's thoughts, or to discuss them with him, or to move the hands of God by prayer. But, strange as it seems, we Christians actually do have within us a portion of the very thoughts and mind of Christ. (1 Corinthians 2:14-16 TLB)

King's kid report: Goo 73-75; Victory 88-89

My personal experience:

Bible. See **Manufacturer's Handbook**
Big-Shot-Itis. See **Self-Reliance**

Billy-Goat Christians
God's answer: I know thy works, that thou art neither cold nor hot: I would thou wert cold or hot. So then because thou art lukewarm, and neither cold nor hot, I will spew thee out of my mouth. (Revelation 3:15-16)

Beware lest any man spoil you through philosophy and vain deceit, after the tradition of men, after the rudiments of the world, and not after Christ. (Colossians 2:8)

King's kid report: Goo 72; Victory 83-89

My personal experience:

Binding And Loosing

God's answer: Verily I say unto you, Whatsoever ye shall bind on earth shall be bound in heaven: and whatsoever ye shall loose on earth shall be loosed in heaven. (Matthew 18:18)

King's kid report: King's Kid 96, 152-55, 207-9; Winner xviii, 85-93; Victory 106-7

My personal experience:

Binding power. See **Atoms**

Blabbermouths

God's answer: Wherefore, my beloved brethren, let every man be swift to hear, slow to speak, slow to wrath. (James 1:19)

And the servant of the Lord must not strive; but must be gentle unto all men, apt to teach, patient, in meekness instructing those that oppose themselves. (2 Timothy 2:24-25a)

But the tongue can no man tame. (James 3:8)

King's kid report: Winner 21-26; Victory 66

My personal experience:

Blahs. See **Emptiness**
Blindness. See **Eyeball Ailments**

Blizzards

God's answer: For he hath said, I will never leave thee, nor forsake thee. (Hebrews 13:5b)

I pray that you will begin to understand how incredibly great his power is to help those who believe him. (Ephesians 1:19 TLB)

King's kid report: Winner 55-61; Victory 11-17, 303-8

My personal experience:

Blown Minds

God's answer: The whole head is sick. (Isaiah 1:5)

But the natural man receiveth not the things of the Spirit of God: for they are foolishness unto him: neither can he know them, because they are spiritually discerned. (1 Corinthians 2:14)

That ye put off concerning the former conversation the old man, which is corrupt according to the deceitful lusts; And be renewed in the spirit of your mind; And that ye put on the new man, which after God is created in righteousness and true holiness. (Ephesians 4:22-24)

King's kid report: Goo 53; Victory 40-46

My personal experience:

Blown tires. See **Highway Accidents**

Bomb Shelters

God's answer: For thou hast been a strength to the poor, a strength to the needy in his distress, a refuge from the storm, a shadow from the heat, when the blast of the terrible ones is as a storm against the wall. (Isaiah 25:4)

King's kid report: King's Kid 144-45

My personal experience:

Boob-Tube-Itis

God's answer: If ye then be risen with Christ, seek those things which are above, where Christ sitteth on the right hand of God. (Colossians 3:1)

Every word of God is pure: he is a shield unto them that put their trust in him. (Proverbs 30:5)

Thy word is a lamp unto my feet, and a light unto my path. (Psalm 119:105)

Let the word of Christ dwell in you richly in all wisdom. (Colossians 3:16a)

Now is the judgment of this world: now shall the prince of this world be cast out. And I, if I be lifted up from the earth, will draw all men unto me. (John 12:31-32)

For a man is a slave to whatever controls him. (2 Peter 2:19b TLB)

King's kid report: Goo 62; Winner 147-48; Victory 136-39, 300

My personal experience:

Boredom. See **Emptiness**

Born Again, How To Be

God's answer: Jesus answered and said unto him, Verily, verily, I say unto thee, Except a man be born again, he cannot see the kingdom of God. (John 3:3)

Only the Holy Spirit gives eternal life. Those born only once, with physical birth, will never receive this gift. (John 6:63 TLB)

But to all who received him, he gave the right to become children of God. All they needed to do was to trust him to save them. All those who believe this are reborn!—not a physical rebirth resulting from human passion or plan—but from the will of God. (John 1:12-13 TLB)

King's kid report: King's Kid 18, 23; Goo 65-69, 80-83, 89-90; Winner 7-14, 195; Victory 151

My personal experience:

Broken Bones

God's answer: We know that all things work together for good to them that love God, to them who are the called according to his purpose. (Romans 8:28)

This sickness is not unto death, but for the glory of God, that the Son of God might be glorified thereby. (John 11:4)

King's kid report: Winner 27-32

My personal experience:

Broken Relationships

God's answer: Therefore if thou bring thy gift to the altar, and there rememberest that thy brother hath ought against thee; leave there thy gift before the altar, and go thy way; first be reconciled to thy brother, and then come and offer thy gift. (Matthew 5:23-24)

And all things are of God, who hath reconciled us to himself by Jesus Christ, and hath given to us the ministry of reconciliation. (2 Corinthians 5:18)

King's kid report: King's Kid 109-11, 200-4; Victory 159, 193-94

My personal experience:

Buddhism, King's Kid 19

Bugaboos. See **Homosexuality**

Bum Rap

God's answer: Offer unto God thanksgiving: and pay thy
vows unto the most High: And call upon me in the day of
trouble: I will deliver thee, and thou shalt glorify me.
(Psalm 50:14-15)

For what glory is it, if, when ye be buffeted for your
faults, ye shall take it patiently? but if, when ye do well,
and suffer for it, ye take it patiently, this is acceptable
with God. (1 Peter 2:20)

King's kid report: Winner 95-100

My personal experience:

Burglary

God's answer: Charge them that are rich in this world, that they be not highminded, nor trust in uncertain riches, but in the living God, who giveth us richly all things to enjoy. (1 Timothy 6:17)

Lay not up for yourselves treasures upon earth, where moth and rust doth corrupt, and where thieves break through and steal: But lay up for yourselves treasures in heaven, where neither moth nor rust doth corrupt, and where thieves do not break through nor steal: For where your treasure is, there will your heart be also. (Matthew 6:19-21)

King's kid report: Winner 55-57, 169-74

My personal experience:

Caleb, Goo 72-3; Victory 32

Cancer

God's answer: My son, attend to my words; incline thine ear unto my sayings. Let them not depart from thine eyes; keep them in the midst of thine heart. For they are life unto those that find them, and health to all their flesh. (Proverbs 4:20-22)

Bless the Lord, O my soul, and forget not all his benefits: who forgiveth all thine iniquities; who healeth all thy diseases. (Psalm 103:2-3)

King's kid report: King's Kid 99-102; Winner 63-69; Victory 63

My personal experience:

Car Trouble (see also **Highway Accidents; Rental Car Shortage; Traffic**)

God's answer: Offer unto God thanksgiving; and pay thy vows unto the most High: And call upon me in the day of trouble: I will deliver thee, and thou shalt glorify me. (Psalm 50:14-15)

I will praise the Lord no matter what happens. (Psalm 34:1 TLB)

Great is his faithfulness; his lovingkindness begins afresh each day. (Lamentations 3:23 TLB)

King's kid report: King's Kid 125-33

My personal experience:

Cayce, Edgar

God's answer: Enter ye in at the strait gate: for wide is the gate, and broad is the way, that leadeth to destruction, and many there be which go in thereat: Because strait is the gate and narrow is the way, which leadeth unto life, and few there be that find it. Beware of false prophets, which come to you in sheep's clothing, but inwardly they are ravening wolves. Ye shall know them by their fruits. (Matthew 7:13-16a)

King's kid report: King's Kid 21, 182; Winner 175-88

My personal experience:

Chaff

God's answer: Whose fan is in his hand, and he will thoroughly purge his floor, and gather his wheat into the garner; but he will burn up the chaff with unquenchable fire. (Matthew 3:12)

The ungodly are not so: but are like the chaff which the wind driveth away. (Psalm 1:4)

King's kid report: Victory 125-27

My personal experience:

Christian Science

God's answer: For many deceivers are entered into the world, who confess not that Jesus Christ is come in the flesh. This is a deceiver and an antichrist. Look to yourselves, that we lose not those things which we have wrought, but that we receive a full reward. Whosoever transgresseth, and abideth not in the doctrine of Christ, hath not God. He that abideth in the doctrine of Christ, he hath both the Father and the Son. (2 John 7-9)

King's kid report: King's Kid 19, 182; Victory 295

My personal experience:

Church Membership

God's answer: And all things are of God, who hath reconciled us to himself by Jesus Christ, and hath given to us the ministry of reconciliation. (2 Corinthians 5:18)

For God is not the author of confusion, but of peace, as in all churches of the saints. (1 Corinthians 14:33)

And they, continuing daily with one accord in the temple, and breaking bread from house to house, did eat their meat with gladness and singleness of heart, Praising God, and having favor with all the people. And the Lord added to the church daily such as should be saved. (Acts 2:46-47)

Not forsaking the assembling of ourselves together, as the manner of some is; but exhorting one another: and so much the more, as ye see the day approaching. (Hebrews 10:25)

King's kid report: King's Kid 142-44; Victory 121-22, 284

My personal experience:

Cirrhosis of the Liver

God's answer: Heal me, O Lord, and I shall be healed; save me, and I shall be saved: for thou art my praise. (Jeremiah 17:14)

But he was wounded for our transgressions, he was bruised for our iniquities: the chastisement of our peace was upon him; and with his stripes we are healed. (Isaiah 53:5)

King's kid report: Winner 101-6, 191-93

My personal experience:

Claiming the Promises (see also **Doers of the Word**)

God's answer: For all the promises of God in him are yea, and in him Amen, unto the glory of God by us. (2 Corinthians 1:20)

God is not a man, that he should lie; neither the son of man, that he should repent: hath he said, and shall he not do it? or hath he spoken, and shall he not make it good? (Numbers 23:19)

King's kid report: King's Kid 150-51; Victory 107

My personal experience:

Clay. See **Potter and the Clay**
Coma, King's Kid 103

Common Sense

God's answer: Why should ye be stricken any more? ye
will revolt more and more: the whole head is sick, and the
whole heart faint. (Isaiah 1:5)

For my thoughts are not your thoughts, neither are your
ways my ways, saith the Lord. (Isaiah 55:8)

King's kid report: King's Kid 133; Victory 46

My personal experience:

Communication gap. See **Language Barrier**

Communion

God's answer: For as often as ye eat this bread, and drink this cup, ye do show the Lord's death till he come. Wherefore whosoever shall eat this bread, and drink this cup of the Lord, unworthily, shall be guilty of the body and blood of the Lord. But let a man examine himself, and so let him eat of that bread, and drink of that cup. For he that eateth and drinketh unworthily, eateth and drinketh damnation to himself, not discerning the Lord's body. For this cause many are weak and sickly among you, and many sleep. (1 Corinthians 11:26-30)

King's kid report: Victory 200-202

My personal experience:

41

Complaining. See **Grumbling**
Computers, King's Kid 66-67, 121

Condemnation (see also **Judging**)
God's answer: There is therefore now no condemnation to
them which are in Christ Jesus, who walk not after the
flesh, but after the Spirit. (Romans 8:1)

King's kid report: Winner 185-86; Victory 61-64, 111-12,
259

My personal experience:

Confession (see also **Negative Confession**)

God's answer: If we confess our sins, he is faithful and just to forgive us our sins, and to cleanse us from all unrighteousness. (1 John 1:9)

Also I say unto you, Whosoever shall confess me before men, him shall the Son of man also confess before the angels of God. (Luke 12:8)

Confess your faults one to another, and pray one for another, that ye may be healed. (James 5:16)

That if thou shalt confess with thy mouth the Lord Jesus, and shalt believe in thine heart that God hath raised him from the dead, thou shalt be saved. For with the heart man believeth unto righteousness; and with the mouth confession is made unto salvation. (Romans 10:9-10)

King's kid report: King's Kid 24, 133-37; Winner 68-69; Victory 62-63, 198-99

My personal experience:

Confucianism, King's Kid 19

Contracts

God's answer: Commit thy works unto the Lord, and thy thoughts shall be established. (Proverbs 16:3)

I will instruct thee and teach thee in the way which thou shalt go: I will guide thee with mine eye. (Psalm 32:8)

Delight thyself also in the Lord: and he shall give thee the desires of thine heart. (Psalm 37:4)

King's kid report: King's Kid 133-37; Victory 266-68

My personal experience:

Corn on the Cob, Victory 255-56
Corpuscle Shortage, Winner 65-68
Creation. See **Evolution vs. Creation**
Crocodiles, King's Kid 193-94

Crooked Friends

God's answer: Vengeance is mine; I will repay, saith the Lord. (Romans 12:19b)

But I say unto you, Love your enemies, bless them that curse you, do good to them that hate you, and pray for them which despitefully use you, and persecute you; That ye may be the children of your Father which is in heaven. (Matthew 5:44-45a)

And the Lord turned the captivity of Job, when he prayed for his friends: also the Lord gave Job twice as much as he had before. (Job 42:10)

King's kid report: Winner 79-83

My personal experience:

Crowded Conditions

God's answers: Pray without ceasing. (1 Thessalonians 5:17)

But my God shall supply all your need according to his riches in glory by Christ Jesus. (Philippians 4:19)

King's kid report: Winner 159-67

My personal experience:

Curtains, Clean, Victory 184-85
Dailey, Starr, King's Kid 85-86
Daniel, Victory 189-91
Darwin. See **Evolution vs. Creation**
David and Bathsheba, Winner 63-69
Death (see also **Graduation Day**), Goo 62-64

Debts

God's answer: And forgive us our debts, as we forgive our debtors. (Matthew 6:12)

For if ye forgive men their trespasses, your heavenly Father will also forgive you: But if ye forgive not men their trespasses, neither will your Father forgive your trespasses. (Matthew 6:14-15)

King's kid report: Winner 79-83; Victory 192-204

My personal experience:

Deceptions. See **Angels of Light; Cayce, Edgar; False Teaching; Fortune Telling; Ouija Boards; Transcendental Meditation**

Deliverance

God's answer: And these signs shall follow them that believe; In my name shall they cast out devils. . . . (Mark 16:17)

But if I cast out devils by the Spirit of God, then the kingdom of God is come unto you. Or else how can one enter into a strong man's house, and spoil his goods, except he first bind the strong man? and then he will spoil his house. (Matthew 12:28-29)

For the accuser of our brethren is cast down, which accused them before our God day and night. And they overcame him by the blood of the Lamb, and by the word of their testimony. (Revelation 12:10b-11)

He sent his word, and healed them, and delivered them from their destructions. (Psalm 107:20)

King's kid report: King's Kid 189-98; Winner 143-49; Victory 91-95

My personal experience:

Demons

God's answer: One cannot rob Satan's kingdom without first binding Satan. Only then can his demons be cast out! (Matthew 12:29 TLB)

And these signs will accompany those who believe; in my name they will cast out demons. (Mark 16:17 RSV)

King's kid report: King's Kid 179-98; Winner 59-61, 143-49, 180-83; Victory 90-95, 196; Goo 53

My personal experience:

Depression

God's answer: He healeth the broken in heart, and bindeth up their wounds. (Psalm 147:3)

Humble yourselves in the sight of the Lord, and he shall lift you up. (James 4:10)

For all the promises of God in him are yea, and in him Amen, unto the glory of God by us. (2 Corinthians 1:20)

For whatsoever is born of God overcometh the world: and this is the victory that overcometh the world, even our faith. Who is he that overcometh the world, but he that believeth that Jesus is the Son of God? (1 John 5:4-5)

The Lord also will be a refuge for the oppressed, a refuge in times of trouble. And they that know thy name will put their trust in thee: for thou, Lord, hast not forsaken them that seek thee. (Psalm 9:9-10)

King's kid report: Winner 143-45; Victory 197, 250-52

My personal experience:

Deserts, Victory 162-65
Devil. See **Satan**
Devils. See **Demons**

Disagreements

God's answer: Therefore if thou bring thy gift to the altar, and there rememberest that thy brother hath ought against thee; leave there thy gift before the altar, and go thy way; first be reconciled to thy brother, and then come and offer thy gift. (Matthew 5:23-24)

Again I say unto you, That if two of you shall agree on earth as touching any thing that they shall ask, it shall be done for them of my Father which is in heaven. (Matthew 18:19)

And all things are of God, who hath reconciled us to himself by Jesus Christ, and hath given to us the ministry of reconciliation. (2 Corinthians 5:18)

King's kid report: Victory 115-17

My personal experience:

Discerning Of Spirits

God's answer: Beloved, believe not every spirit, but try the spirits whether they are of God: because many false prophets are gone out into the world. Hereby know ye the Spirit of God: Every spirit that confesseth that Jesus Christ is come in the flesh is of God: And every spirit that confesseth not that Jesus Christ is come in the flesh is not of God; and this is that spirit of antichrist, whereof ye have heard that it should come; and even now already is it in the world. (1 John 4:1-3)

To another the working of miracles; to another prophecy; to another discerning of spirits. . . . (1 Corinthians 12:10a)

King's kid report: King's Kid 158-65, 193-94; Winner 72, 147, 178; Victory 95, 259, 285

My personal experience:

Discipline

God's answer: My son, do not make light of the Lord's discipline, and do not lose heart when he rebukes you, because the Lord disciplines those whom he loves, and he punishes everyone he accepts as a son. No discipline seems pleasant at the time, but painful. Later on, however, it produces a harvest of righteousness and peace for those who have been trained by it. (Hebrews 12:5-6, 11 NIV)

Ye have not chosen me, but I have chosen you, and ordained you, that ye should go and bring forth fruit, and that your fruit should remain: that whatsoever ye shall ask of the Father in my name, he may give it you. (John 15:16)

Those whom I love I rebuke and discipline. (Revelation 3:19a NIV)

King's kid report: Victory 131-35

My personal experience:

Discouragement (see also **Depression**)

God's answer: For he hath said, I will never leave thee, nor forsake thee. (Hebrews 13:5b)

Nay, in all these things we are more than conquerors through him that loved us. (Romans 8:37)

Being confident of this very thing, that he which hath begun a good work in you will perform it until the day of Jesus Christ. (Philippians 1:6)

Don't be frightened by the size of the task, for the Lord my God is with you: he will not forsake you. He will see to it that everything is finished correctly. (1 Chronicles 28:20b TLB)

Take courage, my soul! Do you remember those times (but how could you ever forget them!) when you led a great procession to the Temple on festival days, singing with joy, praising the Lord? Why then be downcast? Why be discouraged and sad? Hope in God! I shall yet praise him again. Yes, I shall again praise him for his help. (Psalm 42:4-5 TLB)

And let us not get tired of doing what is right, for after a while we will reap a harvest of blessing if we don't get discouraged and give up. (Galatians 6:9 TLB)

King's kid report: Winner xvii-xviii; Victory 30, 227-30

My personal experience:

Disintegrated spinal disk. See **Back Trouble**
Disobedience. See **Rebellion**

Dispensationalism

God's answer: Verily, verily, I say unto you, He that believeth on me, the works that I do shall he do also; and greater works than these shall he do; because I go unto my Father. (John 14:12)

Jesus Christ the same yesterday, and today, and for ever. (Hebrews 13:8)

King's kid report: Winner 102-6; Victory 99-103

My personal experience:

Doers Of The Word

God's answer: For if any be a hearer of the word, and not a doer, he is like unto a man beholding his natural face in a glass: For he beholdeth himself, and goeth his way, and straightway forgetteth what manner of man he was. But whoso looketh into the perfect law of liberty, and continueth therein, he being not a forgetful hearer, but a doer of the work, this man shall be blessed in his deed. (James 1:23-25)

The Kingdom of God is not just talking; it is living by God's power. (1 Corinthians 4:20 TLB)

Yes, but even more blessed are all who hear the Word of God and put it into practice. (Luke 11:28 TLB)

King's kid report: King's Kid 102-5, 116-17; Winner 87-92; Victory 11-23, 96-98, 219-21, 238-39; Goo 89

My personal experience:

Dogs, Training Of, Victory 265

Doing God's Will
  God's answer: Rejoice evermore. Pray without ceasing.
  In everything give thanks: for this is the will of God in
  Christ Jesus concerning you. (1 Thessalonians 5:16-18)

  And be not conformed to this world: but be ye transformed
  by the renewing of your mind, that ye may prove what is
  that good, and acceptable, and perfect, will of God.
  (Romans 12:2)

  King's kid report: Victory 68-74, 299-300

  My personal experience:

Doublemindedness. See **Singlemindedness**
Downing, Frank, King's Kid 143

Drinking Too Much

God's answer: He himself gives life and breath to everything and satisfies every need there is. (Acts 17:25b TLB)

My grace is sufficient for thee: for my strength is made perfect in weakness. (2 Corinthians 12:9a)

All things are lawful unto me, but all things are not expedient: all things are lawful for me, but I will not be brought under the power of any. (1 Corinthians 6:12)

And be not drunk with wine, wherein is excess; but be filled with the Spirit. (Ephesians 5:18)

King's kid report: King's Kid 11-16; Winner 191-93; Victory 1-10, 12-14

My personal experience:

Drugs. See **Drinking Too Much; Heroin; LSD; Smoking**
Dry Bones, Winner 66-68
Eagles, Victory 213-15

Educated Idiots And The Educated Idiot Box

God's answer: For God says, "I will destroy all human plans of salvation no matter how wise they seem to be, and ignore the best ideas of men, even the most brilliant of them." So what about these wise men, these scholars, these brilliant debaters of this world's great affairs? God has made them all look foolish, and shown their wisdom to be useless nonsense. For God in his wisdom saw to it that the world would never find God through human brilliance, and then he stepped in and saved all those who believed his message, which the world calls foolish and silly. (1 Corinthians 1:19-21 TLB)

Verily I say unto you, Except ye be converted, and become as little children, ye shall not enter into the kingdom of heaven. (Matthew 18:3)

But God hath chosen the foolish things of the world to confound the wise; and God hath chosen the weak things of the world to confound the things which are mighty; And base things of the world, and things which are despised, hath God chosen, yea, and things which are not, to bring to nought things that are: That no flesh should glory in his presence. (1 Corinthians 1:27-29)

Stop fooling yourselves. If you count yourself above average in intelligence, as judged by this world's standards, you had better put this all aside and be a fool rather than let it hold you back from the true wisdom from above. For the wisdom of this world is foolishness to God.

As it says in the book of Job, God uses man's own brilliance to trap him; he stumbles over his own "wisdom" and falls. And again, in the book of Psalms, we are told that the Lord knows full well how the human mind reasons, and how foolish and futile it is. (1 Corinthians 3:18-20 TLB)

King's kid report: King's Kid xi, 6-7, 181-82; Goo 67; Winner 31, 102; Victory 41, 105, 240-49

My personal experience:

Ego Trips

God's answer: Let nothing be done through strife or vainglory; but in lowliness of mind let each esteem other better than themselves. Look not every man on his own things, but every man also on the things of others. (Philippians 2:3-4)

But he that is greatest among you shall be your servant. And whosoever shall exalt himself shall be abased; and he that shall humble himself shall be exalted. (Matthew 23:11-12)

But he that glorieth, let him glory in the Lord. For not he that commendeth himself is approved, but whom the Lord commendeth. (2 Corinthians 10:17-18)

He that speaketh of himself seeketh his own glory: but he that seeketh his glory that sent him, the same is true, and no unrighteousness is in him. (John 7:18)

The Lord says: Let not the wise man bask in his wisdom, nor the mighty man in his might, nor the rich man in his riches. Let them boast in this alone: That they truly know me, and understand that I am the Lord of justice and of righteousness whose love is steadfast; and that I love to be this way. (Jeremiah 9:23-24 TLB)

King's kid report: Victory 11-17

My personal experience:

Emptiness

God's answer: My heart and my flesh crieth out for the living God. (Psalm 84:2b)

And ye are complete in him, which is the head of all principality and power. (Colossians 2:10)

I am come that they might have life, and that they might have it more abundantly. (John 10:10b)

And ye shall seek me, and find me, when ye shall search for me with all your heart. (Jeremiah 29:13)

Look! I have been standing at the door and I am constantly knocking. If anyone hears me calling him and opens the door, I will come in and fellowship with him and he with me. (Revelation 3:20 TLB)

And to know the love of Christ, which passeth knowledge, that ye might be filled with all the fulness of God. (Ephesians 3:19)

Yes, everything else is worthless when compared with the priceless gain of knowing Christ Jesus my Lord. I have put aside all else, counting it worth less than nothing, in order that I can have Christ. (Philippians 3:8-9 TLB)

King's kid report: King's Kid 9-12, 16-17, 73-74; Goo 66; Winner 12-14, 74-77; Victory 76-78, 217-221

My personal experience:

Eternal life. See **Born Again, How to Be**

Eve. See **Adam and Eve**

Evolution vs. Creation

God's answer: And God created great whales, and every living creature that moveth, which the waters brought forth abundantly, after their kind, and every winged fowl after his kind: and God saw that it was good. And God said, Let the earth bring forth the living creature after his kind, cattle, and crreeping thing, and beast of the earth after his kind: and it was so. And God said, Let us make man in our image, after our likeness. (Genesis 1:21, 24, 26a)

All flesh is not the same flesh: but there is one kind of flesh of men, another flesh of beasts, another of fishes, and another of birds. (1 Corinthians 15:39)

Through faith we understand that the worlds were framed by the word of God, so that things which are seen were not made of things which do appear. (Hebrews 11:3)

In the beginning was the Word, and the Word was with God, and the Word was God. The same was in the beginning with God. All things were made by him; and without him was not any thing made that was made. (John 1:1-3)

King's kid report: King's Kid 20; Goo ix-104

My personal experience:

Exorcism. See **Demons**

Eyeball Ailments

God's answer: Heal me, O Lord, and I shall be healed; save me, and I shall be saved: for thou art my praise. (Jeremiah 17:14)

The Lord will perfect that which concerneth me: thy mercy, O Lord, endureth forever. (Psalm 138:8a)

The Spirit of the Lord is upon me, because he hath anointed me to preach the gospel to the poor; he hath sent me to heal the brokenhearted, to preach deliverance to the captives, and recovering of sight to the blind, to set at liberty them that are bruised. (Luke 4:18)

King's kid report: Victory 107-10, 115-17

My personal experience:

Eyeball Guidance

God's answer: I will instruct thee and teach thee in the way which thou shalt go: I will guide thee with mine eye. (Psalm 32:8)

King's kid report: Victory 263-65

My personal experience:

Faith

God's answer: Now faith is the substance of things hoped for, the evidence of things not seen. (Hebrews 11:1)

For whatsoever is born of God overcometh the world: and this is the victory that overcometh the world, even our faith. (1 John 5:4)

So then faith cometh by hearing, and hearing by the word of God. (Romans 10:17)

And Jesus said unto them, Because of your unbelief: for verily I say unto you, If ye have faith as a grain of mustard seed, ye shall say unto this mountain, Remove hence to yonder place; and it shall remove; and nothing shall be impossible unto you. (Matthew 17:20)

God hath dealt to every man the measure of faith. (Romans 12:3b)

King's kid report: King's Kid 101-2, 191-92; Winner 102-3; Victory 25-39, 112-14, 234-35

My personal experience:

False Teaching (see also **Cayce, Edgar; Christian Science; Evolution vs. Creation; Jehovah's Witnesses; Transcendental Meditation; Unity; Universalism**)

God's answer: Now the Spirit speaketh expressly, that in the later times some shall depart from the faith, giving heed to seducing spirits, and doctrines and devils. (1 Timothy 4:1)

That we henceforth be no more children, tossed to and fro, and carried about with every wind of doctrine, by the sleight of men, and cunning craftiness, whereby they lie in wait to deceive; But speaking the truth in love, may grow up into him in all things, which is the head, even Christ. (Ephesians 4:14-15)

Beloved, believe not every spirit, but try the spirits whether they are of God: because many false prophets are gone out into the world. Hereby know ye the Spirit of God: Every spirit that confesseth that Jesus Christ is come in the flesh is of God: And every spirit that confesseth not that Jesus Christ is come in the flesh is not of God; and this is that spirit of antichrist, whereof ye have heard that it should come; and even now already is it in the world. (1 John 4:1-3)

O foolish Galatians, who hath bewitched you, that ye should not obey the truth, before whose eyes Jesus Christ hath been evidently set forth, crucified among you? (Galatians 3:1)

King's kid report: King's Kid 19-21; Victory 281-300;
Winner 178

My personal experience:

Family, Salvation of

God's answer: Likewise, ye wives, be in subjection to your own husbands; that, if any obey not the word, they also may without the word be won by the conversation of the wives; While they behold your chaste conversation coupled with fear. (1 Peter 3:1-2)

Believe on the Lord Jesus Christ, and thou shalt be saved, and thy house. (Acts 16:31)

King's kid report: King's Kid 150-51; Victory 179-80

My personal experience:

Fault-finding. See **Grumbling**

Fear

God's answer: For God hath not given us the spirit of fear; but of power, and of love, and of a sound mind. (2 Timothy 1:7)

I sought the Lord, and he heard me, and delivered me from all my fears. (Psalm 34:4)

Fear thou not; for I am with thee: be not dismayed; for I am thy God: I will strengthen thee; yea, I will help thee; yea, I will uphold thee with the right hand of my righteousness. (Isaiah 41:10)

The fear of man bringeth a snare: but whoso putteth his trust in the Lord shall be safe. (Proverbs 29:25)

And the Lord, he it is that doth go before thee; he will be with thee, he will not fail thee, neither forsake thee: fear not, neither be dismayed. (Deuteronomy 31:8)

There is no fear in love; but perfect love casteth out fear: because fear hath torment. He that feareth is not made perfect in love. (1 John 4:18)

King's kid report: King's Kid 185-87; Goo 76; Winner vii; Victory 222-24, 253-54

My personal experience:

Feelings

God's answer: Judge not according to the appearance, but judge righteous judgment. (John 7:24)

Do ye look on things after the outward appearance? If any man trust to himself that he is Christ's, let him of himself think this again, that, as he is Christ's, even so are we Christ's. (2 Corinthians 10:7)

For we walk by faith, not by sight. (2 Corinthians 5:7)

King's kid report: Winner 15, 21, 130; Victory 25-30, 73, 151, 155-56, 184-87

My personal experience:

Firebombs

God's answer: The fear of man bringeth a snare: but whoso putteth his trust in the Lord shall be safe. (Proverbs 29:25)

Fear ye not, stand still, and see the salvation of the Lord, which he will shew to you today. (Exodus 14:13)

King's kid report: King's Kid 117-20

My personal experience:

Fish, Victory 21-22
Fishing, Winner 136-41; Victory 147-48
Flat Tires, Victory 15

Flattened Billfold

God's answer: And on the morrow when he departed, he
took out two pence, and gave them to the host, and said
unto him, Take care of him; and whatsoever thou spendest
more, when I come again, I will repay thee. (Luke 10:35)

King's kid report: Victory 13-17

My personal experience:

Fleeces

God's answer: And he said unto him, If now I have found grace in thy sight, then shew me a sign that thou talkest with me. (Judges 6:17)

Behold, I will put a fleece of wool in the floor, and if the dew be on the fleece only, and it be dry upon all the earth beside, then shall I know that thou wilt save Israel by mine hand, as thou hast said. (Judges 6:37)

King's kid report: King's Kid 206; Winner 113-14; Victory 167-72

My personal experience:

Fog

God's answer: For now we see through a glass, darkly; but then face to face: now I know in part; but then shall I know even as also I am known. (1 Corinthians 13:12)

For we walk by faith, not by sight. (2 Corinthians 5:7)

King's kid report: King's Kid 139-42

My personal experience:

Footnote Theology, Victory 90-98

Forgiveness (see also **Unforgiveness**)

God's answer: So overflowing is his kindness towards us that he took away all our sins through the blood of his Son, by whom we are saved. (Ephesians 1:7 TLB)

But if we walk in the light, as he is in the light, we have fellowship one with another, and the blood of Jesus Christ his Son cleanseth us from all sin. (1 John 1:7)

In fact we can say that under the old agreement almost everything was cleansed by sprinkling it with blood, and without the shedding of blood there is no forgiveness of sins. (Hebrews 9:22 TLB)

Having therefore, brethren, boldness to enter into the holiest by the blood of Jesus. (Hebrews 10:19)

King's kid report: King's Kid 17-18, 24; Winner 66-69

My personal experience:

Fouled-Up Flight Plans

God's answer: And we know that all things work together for good to them that love God, to them who are the called according to his purpose. (Romans 8:28)

Rest in the Lord, and wait patiently for him. (Psalm 37:7a)

King's kid report: King's Kid 1-6, 139-42; Winner 151-57

My personal experience:

Fruit-Bearing

God's answer: And the cares of this world, and the deceitfulness of riches, and the lusts of other things entering in, choke the word, and it becometh unfruitful. (Mark 4:19)

But his delight is in the law of the Lord; and in his law doth he meditate day and night. And he shall be like a tree planted by the rivers of water, that bringeth forth his fruit in his season; his leaf also shall not wither; and whatsoever he doeth shall prosper. (Psalm 1:2-3)

Abide in me, and I in you. As the branch cannot bear fruit of itself, except it abide in the vine; no more can ye, except ye abide in me. (John 15:4)

Ye have not chosen me, but I have chosen you, and ordained you, that ye should go and bring forth fruit, and that your fruit should remain: that whatsoever ye shall ask of the Father in my name, he may give it you. (John 15:16)

King's kid report: Victory 121-35

My personal experience:

79

Frustration

God's answer: Now thanks be unto God, which always causeth us to triumph in Christ. (2 Corinthians 2:14a)

I can do all things through Christ which strengtheneth me. (Philippians 4:13)

My grace is sufficient for thee: for my strength is made perfect in weakness. Most gladly therefore will I rather glory in my infirmities, that the power of Christ may rest upon me. (2 Corinthians 12:9)

Greater is he that is in you, than he that is in the world. (1 John 4:4b)

King's kid report: Goo 86; Victory 42

My personal experience:

Fullness of Time

God's answer: But when the fulness of the time was come, God sent forth his Son, made of a woman, made under the law. (Galatians 4:4)

That in the dispensation of the fulness of times he might gather together in one all things in Christ, both which are in heaven, and which are on earth; even in him. (Ephesians 1:10)

King's kid report: Victory 110, 127

My personal experience:

Furry Things, King's Kid 196-97

Gambling

God's answer: Set your affection on things above, not on things on the earth. (Colossians 3:2)

And have no fellowship with the unfruitful works of darkness, but rather reprove them. (Ephesians 5:11)

All things are lawful for me, but all things are not expedient: all things are lawful for me, but all things edify not. (1 Corinthians 10:23)

For a man is a slave to whatever controls him. (2 Peter 2:19b TLB)

King's kid report: King's Kid 27-29

My personal experience:

Gifts of the Holy Spirit

God's answer: Verily, verily, I say unto you, He that believeth on me, the works that I do shall he do also; and greater works than these shall he do; because I go unto my Father. (John 14:12)

Every good gift and every perfect gift is from above, and cometh down from the Father of lights, with whom is no variableness, neither shadow of turning. (James 1:17)

For God's gifts and his call can never be withdrawn; he will never go back on his promises. (Romans 11:29 TLB)

Now you have every grace and blessing; every spiritual gift and power for doing his will are yours during this time of waiting for the return of our Lord Jesus Christ. (1 Corinthians 1:7 TLB)

Now there are diversities of gifts, but the same Spirit. (1 Corinthians 12:4)

King's kid report: King's Kid 104-5; Winner 184; Victory 231-40, 269-75

My personal experience:

Glory meter. See **Liebman's Glory Meter**
God's will. See **Doing God's Will**
Good for nothing. See **Unworthiness**

Good Works (see also **Programitis**)

God's answer: And then there is your "righteousness" and your "good works"—none of which will save you. (Isaiah 57:12 TLB)

Not by works of righteousness which we have done, but according to his mercy he saved us, by the washing of regeneration, and renewing of the Holy Ghost. (Titus 3:5)

For by grace are ye saved through faith; and that not of yourselves: it is the gift of God: Not of works, lest any man should boast. (Ephesians 2:8-9)

But we are all as an unclean thing, and all our righteousnesses are as filthy rags. (Isaiah 64:6a)

King's kid report: King's Kid 24; Victory 80, 295

My personal experience:

Gossip

God's answer: If any man among you seem to be religious, and bridleth not his tongue, but deceiveth his own heart, this man's religion is vain. (James 1:26)

Only let your conversation be as it becometh the gospel of Christ. (Philippians 1:27a)

The words of a talebearer are as wounds, and they go down into the innermost parts of the belly. (Proverbs 18:8)

King's kid report: King's Kid 81-87, 195

My personal experience:

Graduation Day

God's answer: Jesus said unto her, I am the resurrection, and the life: he that believeth in me, though he were dead, yet shall he live: And whosoever liveth and believeth in me shall never die. (John 11:25-26)

Death is swallowed up in victory. . . . But thanks be to God, which giveth us the victory through our Lord Jesus Christ. (1 Corinthians 15:54b, 57)

Therefore we are always confident, knowing that, whilst we are at home in the body, we are absent from the Lord: (For we walk by faith, not by sight:) We are confident, I say, and willing rather to be absent from the body, and to be present with the Lord. (2 Corinthians 5:6-8)

Yea, though I walk through the valley of the shadow of death, I will fear no evil: for thou art with me. (Psalm 23:4)

Verily, verily, I say unto you, If a man keep my saying, he shall never see death. (John 8:51)

For this purpose the Son of God was manifested, that he might destroy the works of the devil. (1 John 3:8b)

King's kid report: King's Kid 121-22, 147-49; Winner 189-91; Victory 157-58, 191

My personal experience:

Grapevines

God's answer: But his delight is in the law of the Lord; and in his law doth he meditate day and night. And he shall be like a tree planted by the rivers of water, that bringeth forth his fruit in his season; his leaf also shall not wither; and whatsoever he doeth shall prosper. (Psalm 1:2-3)

King's kid report: Victory 131-35

My personal experience:

Gravity, Winner 9-10
Ground Energizer, Winner 49-53
Grounded Planes, Winner 49-53

Grumbling

God's answer: Do all things without murmurings and disputings: that ye may be blameless and harmless, the sons of God, without rebuke, in the midst of a crooked and perverse nation, among whom ye shine as lights in the world. (Philippians 2:14-15)

Fix your thoughts on what is true and good and right. Think about things that are pure and lovely, and dwell on the fine, good things in others. Think about all you can praise God for and be glad about. (Philippians 4:8 TLB)

For ye were sometimes darkness, but now are ye light in the Lord: walk as children of light. (Ephesians 5:8)

And when the people complained, it displeased the Lord. (Numbers 11:1a)

King's kid report: King's Kid 207; Victory 69-70, 108

My personal experience:

Guidance (see also **Eyeball Guidance**)

God's answer: Let the word of Christ dwell in you richly in all wisdom. (Colossians 3:16a)

As newborn babes, desire the sincere milk of the word, that ye may grow thereby. (1 Peter 2:2)

Thy word is a lamp unto my feet, and a light unto my path. (Psalm 119:105)

These things that were written in the Scriptures so long ago are to teach us. (Romans 15:4 TLB)

Call unto me, and I will answer thee, and show thee great and mighty things, which thou knowest not. (Jeremiah 33:3)

For this God is our God for ever and ever: he will be our guide even unto death. (Psalm 48:14)

Commit thy works unto the Lord, and thy thoughts shall be established. (Proverbs 16:3)

King's kid report: Victory 155-56, 263-68

My personal experience:

Guilt

God's answer: Brothers! Listen! In this man Jesus, there is forgiveness for your sins! Everyone who trusts in him is freed from all guilt and declared righteous. (Acts 13:38-39 TLB)

If we confess our sins, he is faithful and just to forgive us our sins, and to cleanse us from all unrighteousness. (1 John 1:9)

Come now, and let us reason together, saith the Lord: though your sins be as scarlet, they shall be as white as snow; though they be red like crimson, they shall be as wool. (Isaiah 1:18)

So overflowing is his kindness towards us that he took away all our sins through the blood of his Son, by whom we are saved. (Ephesians 1:7 TLB)

King's kid report: Goo 75; King's Kid 18, 23-24, 201-2; Winner 63-69; Victory 198

My personal experience:

Harvest

God's answer: Pray ye therefore the Lord of the harvest, that he will send forth labourers into his harvest. (Matthew 9:38)

And he saith unto them, Follow me, and I will make you fishers of men. (Matthew 4:19)

Not by might, nor by power, but by my spirit, saith the Lord of hosts. (Zechariah 4:6b)

King's kid report: Victory 143-48

My personal experience:

Head-on collisions. See **Highway Accidents**

Healing (see also **Communion; Laying On of Hands:** and names of specific ailments, e.g., **Arthritis, Back Trouble, Cancer,** etc.)

God's answer: Is any sick among you? let him call for the elders of the church; and let them pray over him, anointing him with oil in the name of the Lord: And the prayer of faith shall save the sick, and the Lord shall raise him up; and if he have committed sins, they shall be forgiven him. (James 5:14-15)

I pray that you will begin to understand how incredibly great his power is to help those who believe him. (Ephesians 1:19 TLB)

But he was wounded for our transgressions, he was bruised for our iniquities: the chastisement of our peace was upon him; and with his stripes we are healed. (Isaiah 53:5)

And heal the sick that are therein, and say unto them, The kingdom of God is come nigh unto you. (Luke 10:9)

For I will restore health unto thee, and I will heal thee of thy wounds, saith the Lord. (Jeremiah 30:17a)

King's kid report: King's Kid 99-112; Victory 105-17, 234

My personal experience:

Heart Trouble

God's answer: Men's hearts failing them for fear, and for looking after those things which are coming on the earth. (Luke 21:26a)

Wherefore as the Holy Ghost saith, Today if ye will hear his voice, Harden not your hearts, as in the provocation, in the day of temptation in the wilderness. (Hebrews 3:7-8)

Come unto me, all ye that labour and are heavy laden, and I will give you rest. Take my yoke upon you, and learn of me; for I am meek and lowly in heart: and ye shall find rest unto your souls. For my yoke is easy, and my burden is light. (Matthew 11:28-30)

A new heart also will I give you, and a new spirit will I put within you: and I will take away the stony heart out of your flesh, and I will give you an heart of flesh. (Ezekiel 36:26)

King's kid report: Goo 75-77; Winner 189-93

My personal experience:

Heroin

God's answer: For because he himself has suffered and been tempted, he is able to help those who are tempted. (Hebrews 2:18 RSV)

There hath no temptation taken you but such as is common to man: but God is faithful, who will not suffer you to be tempted above that ye are able; but will with the temptation also make a way to escape, that ye may be able to bear it. (1 Corinthians 10:13)

I will praise thee with my whole heart. . . . In the day when I cried thou answeredst me, and strengthenedst me with strength in my soul. (Psalm 138:1a, 3)

King's kid report: Winner 39-47

My personal experience:

Hezekiah, King's Kid 68-69

Highway Accidents
God's answer: Fear thou not; for I am with thee: be not dismayed; for I am thy God: I will strengthen thee; yea, I will help thee; yea, I will uphold thee with the right hand of my righteousness. (Isaiah 41:10)

And the Lord, he it is that doth go before thee; he will be with thee, he will not fail thee, neither forsake thee: fear not, neither be dismayed. (Deuteronomy 31:8)

Then they cried unto the Lord in their trouble, and he delivered them out of their distresses. (Psalm 107:6)

King's kid report: King's Kid 112-16, 147-49

My personal experience:

Hinduism, King's Kid 20
Hippopotamus, King's Kid 193-94

Holy Spirit (see also **Baptism in the Holy Spirit; Gifts of the Holy Spirit**)

God's answer: But the Comforter, which is the Holy Ghost, whom the Father will send in my name, he shall teach you all things, and bring all things to your remembrance, whatsoever I have said unto you. (John 14:26)

Even the Spirit of truth; whom the world cannot receive, because it seeth him not, neither knoweth him: but ye know him: for he dwelleth with you, and shall be in you. (John 14:17)

But ye shall receive power, after that the Holy Ghost is come upon you: and ye shall be witnesses unto me both in Jerusalem and in all Judea, and in Samaria, and unto the uttermost part of the earth. (Acts 1:8)

King's kid report: King's Kid 47; Goo 79-90; Winner 17-20

My personal experience:

Homosexuality

God's answer: Those who live immoral lives, who are idol worshipers, adulterers or homosexuals—will have no share in his kingdom. . . . There was a time when some of you were just like that but now your sins are washed away, and you are set apart for God, and he has accepted you because of what the Lord Jesus Christ and the Spirit of our God have done for you. (1 Corinthians 6:10-11 TLB)

Wherefore God also gave them up to uncleanness through the lusts of their own hearts, to dishonor their own bodies between themselves: Who changed the truth of God into a lie, and worshipped and served the creature more than the Creator, who is blessed for ever. Amen. For this cause God gave them up unto vile affections: for even their women did change the natural use into that which is against nature: And likewise also the men, leaving the natural use of the woman, burned in their lust one toward another; men with men working that which is unseemly, and receiving in themselves that recompence of their error which was meet. (Romans 1:24-27)

King's kid report: Winner 59-60

My personal experience:

Horoscopes

God's answer: Don't act like the people who make horoscopes and try to read their fate and the future in the stars! Don't be frightened by predictions such as theirs, for it is all a pack of lies. Their ways are futile and foolish. (Jeremiah 10:2-3 TLB)

King's kid report: King's Kid 182; Winner 149, 183, 187-88; Victory 296

My personal experience:

Hot line to heaven. See **Tongues**
Hotel No-Vacancy Signs, Winner 113-20; Victory 227-30
Hurricanes, Victory 219-21

Husband-Wife Haggles

God's answer: Wives, submit yourselves unto your own husbands, as unto the Lord. For the husband is the head of the wife, even as Christ is the head of the church: and he is the saviour of the body. Therefore as the church is subject unto Christ, so let the wives be to their own husbands in everything. (Ephesians 5:22-24)

Husbands, love your wives, even as Christ also loved the church, and gave himself for it; That he might sanctify and cleanse it with the washing of water by the word, That he might present it to himself a glorious church, not having spot, or wrinkle, or any such thing: but that it should be holy and without blemish. So ought men to love their wives as their own bodies. He that loveth his wife loveth himself. (Ephesians 5:25-28)

King's kid report: Victory 173-85, 193-94

My personal experience:

Icky Prayer List, Winner 185; Victory 89
Iffy doctrines. See **False Teaching**

Ignorance

God's answer: For they being ignorant of God's righteousness, and going about to establish their own righteousness, have not submitted themselves unto the righteousness of God. (Romans 10:3)

Having the understanding darkened, being alienated from the life of God through the ignorance that is in them, because of the blindness of their heart. (Ephesians 4:18)

But the natural man receiveth not the things of the Spirit of God: for they are foolishness unto him: neither can he know them, because they are spiritually discerned. But he that is spiritual judgeth all things, yet he himself is judged of no man. (1 Corinthians 2:14-15)

Now concerning spiritual gifts, brethren, I would not have you ignorant. (1 Corinthians 12:1)

King's kid report: King's Kid 173; Victory 84, 269-75

My personal experience:

Impatience

God's answer: Don't be impatient for the Lord to act! Keep traveling steadily along his pathway and in due season he will honor you with every blessing. (Psalm 37:34 TLB)

Wherefore seeing we also are compassed about with so great a cloud of witnesses, let us lay aside every weight, and the sin which doth so easily beset us, and let us run with patience the race that is set before us, Looking unto Jesus the author and finisher of our faith. (Hebrews 12:1-2a)

Strengthened with all might, according to his glorious power, unto all patience and longsuffering with joyfulness. (Colossians 1:11)

But the fruit of the Spirit is love, joy, peace, patience, kindness, goodness, faithfulness, gentleness and self-control. (Galatians 5:22 RSV)

King's kid report: Winner 16, 153; Victory 57-58, 127, 154-55, 205-11

My personal experience:

Iniquity. See **Guilt**

Insanity

God's answer: These things I have spoken unto you, that in me ye might have peace. In the world ye shall have tribulation: but be of good cheer; I have overcome the world. (John 16:33)

For whatsoever is born of God overcometh the world: and this is the victory that overcometh the world, even our faith. Who is he that overcometh the world, but he that believeth that Jesus is the Son of God. (1 John 5:4-5)

I will not leave you comfortless: I will come to you. (John 14:18)

King's kid report: King's Kid 181-83; 189-95

My personal experience:

Intercessory prayer. See **Prayer, Intercessory**

Intensive Care

God's answer: Casting all your care upon him; for he
careth for you. (1 Peter 5:7)

We know that all things work together for good to them
that love God, to them who are the called according to his
purpose. (Romans 8:28)

He will listen to the prayers of the destitute, for he is
never too busy to heed their requests. (Psalm 102:17 TLB)

King's kid report: Winner 191-93

My personal experience:

Interpretation of Tongues

God's answer: Wherefore let him that speaketh in an unknown tongue pray that he may interpret. What is it then? I will pray with the spirit, and I will pray with the understanding also: I will sing with the spirit, and I will sing with the understanding also. (1 Corinthians 14:13, 15)

King's kid report: King's Kid 136, 158, 194; Victory 235

My personal experience:

Inventions. See **Ground Energizer**

Jehovah's Witnesses

God's answer: But there were false prophets also among
the people, even as there shall be false teachers among
you, who privily shall bring in damnable heresies, even
denying the Lord that bought them, and bring upon
themselves swift destruction. And many shall follow their
pernicious ways; by reason of whom the way of truth shall
be evil spoken of. (2 Peter 2:1-2)

King's kid report: King's Kid 59-63

My personal experience:

Jeremiah, Victory 53-54
Jewish Spiritists, Winner 71-77
Job, Victory 112, 160-61
Job loss. See **Unemployment**
Joshua, King's Kid 66-67; Goo 72-73; Victory 32

Judging

God's answer: Therefore thou art inexcusable, O man, whosoever thou art that judgest: for wherein thou judgest another, thou condemnest thyself; for thou that judgest doest the same things. (Romans 2:1)

And why beholdest thou the mote that is in thy brother's eye, but considerest not the beam that is in thine own eye? (Matthew 7:3)

King's kid report: Victory 65-67, 258-59

My personal experience:

Knowledge. See **Word Of Knowledge**
Lack of power. See **Power Shortage**

Landing-Gear Malfunction

God's answer: Rejoice evermore. Pray without ceasing. In everything give thanks: for this is the will of God in Christ Jesus concerning you. (1 Thessalonians 5:16-18)

Have not I commanded thee? Be strong and of a good courage; be not afraid, neither be thou dismayed: for the Lord thy God is with thee whithersoever thou goest. (Joshua 1:9)

King's kid report: King's Kid 1-6

My personal experience:

Language Barrier

God's answer: But whatsoever shall be given you in that hour, that speak ye: for it is not ye that speak, but the Holy Ghost. (Mark 13:11b)

For the Holy Ghost shall teach you in the same hour what ye ought to say. (Luke 12:12)

Trust in the Lord with all thine heart; and lean not unto thine own understanding. In all thy ways acknowledge him, and he shall direct thy paths. (Proverbs 3:5-6)

Open thy mouth wide, and I will fill it. (Psalm 81:10b)

King's kid report: King's Kid 85-87; Winner 1-8, 130-32

My personal experience:

Laser Beam

God's answer: For the word of God is quick, and powerful, and sharper than any two-edged sword, piercing even to the dividing asunder of soul and spirit, and of the joints and marrow, and is a discerner of the thoughts and intents of the heart. (Hebrews 4:12)

King's kid report: Victory 37-39

My personal experience:

Lawsuits

God's answer: If we confess our sins, he is faithful and just to forgive us our sins, and to cleanse us from all unrighteousness. (1 John 1:9)

Offer unto God thanksgiving; and pay thy vows unto the most High: And call upon me in the day of trouble: I will deliver thee, and thou shalt glorify me. (Psalm 50:14-15)

King's kid report: King's Kid 133-37; Winner 80-82

My personal experience:

Laying on of Hands

God's answer: These signs shall follow them that believe; In my name . . . they shall lay hands on the sick, and they shall recover. (Mark 16:17-18)

King's kid report: King's Kid 39-40, 99-105, 175-77; Winner 30, 101-6; Victory 97-98, 102-3, 237

My personal experience:

Leukemia, Winner 64-69
Liebman's Glory Meter, Goo 81-86

Light

God's answer: Then spake Jesus again unto them, saying,
I am the light of the world: he that followeth me shall not
walk in darkness, but shall have the light of life. (John
8:12)

But if we walk in the light, as he is in the light, we have
fellowship one with another, and the blood of Jesus Christ
his Son cleanseth us from all sin. (1 John 1:7)

For ye were sometimes darkness, but now are ye light in
the Lord: walk as children of light. (Ephesians 5:8)

And the city had no need of the sun, neither of the moon, to
shine in it: for the glory of God did lighten it, and the Lamb
is the light thereof. (Revelation 21:23)

King's kid report: Goo 22-23, 82, 86-89; King's Kid 116;
Winner 180; Victory 95, 300

My personal experience:

Lions, Victory 189-91

Lost in Strange Surroundings
God's answer: Yes, be bold and strong! Banish fear and doubt! For remember, the Lord your God is with you wherever you go. (Joshua 1:9 TLB)

If any of you lack wisdom, let him ask of God . . . and it shall be given him. (James 1:5)

And thine ears shall hear a word behind thee, saying, This is the way, walk ye in it, when ye turn to the right hand, and when ye turn to the left. (Isaiah 30:21)

King's kid report: Winner 127-33; Victory 309-12

My personal experience:

Love

God's answer: Now you can have real love for everyone because your souls have been cleansed from selfishness and hatred when you trusted Christ to save you; so see to it that you really do love each other warmly, with all your hearts. (1 Peter 1:22 TLB)

The love of God is shed abroad in our hearts by the Holy Ghost which is given unto us. (Romans 5:5b)

And the Lord make you to increase and abound in love one toward another, and toward all men, even as we do toward you. (1 Thessalonians 3:12)

But when the Holy Spirit controls our lives he will produce this kind of fruit in us: love. . . . (Galatians 5:22 TLB)

He that loveth not knoweth not God; for God is love. (1 John 4:8)

And to know the love of Christ, which passeth knowledge, that ye might be filled with all the fulness of God. (Ephesians 3:19)

King's kid report: King's Kid 56; Victory 84-87, 181-82

My personal experience:

LSD

God's answer: All things are lawful unto me, but all things are not expedient: all things are lawful for me, but I will not be brought under the power of any. (1 Corinthians 6:12)

Be sober, be vigilant; because your adversary the devil, as a roaring lion, walketh about, seeking whom he may devour. (1 Peter 5:8)

Now thanks be unto God, which always causeth us to triumph in Christ, and maketh manifest the savor of his knowledge by us in every place. (2 Corinthians 2:14)

Greater is he that is in you, than he that is in the world. (1 John 4:4b)

King's kid report: Winner 146

My personal experience:

Lust

God's answer: For all that is in the world, the lust of the flesh, and the lust of the eyes, and the pride of life, is not of the Father, but is of the world. (1 John 2:16)

King's kid report: Victory 77

My personal experience:

Machinery repair. See **Technical Difficulties**

Manifest Sons of God

God's answer: Beloved, believe not every spirit, but try the spirits whether they are of God: because many false prophets are gone out into the world. Hereby know ye the Spirit of God: Every spirit that confesseth that Jesus Christ is come in the flesh is of God: And every spirit that confesseth not that Jesus Christ is come in the flesh is not of God: and this is that spirit of antichrist, whereof ye have heard that it should come; and even now already is it in the world. Ye are of God, little children, and have overcome them: because greater is he that is in you, than he that is in the world. They are of the world: therefore speak they of the world, and the world heareth them. We are of God: he that knoweth God heareth us; he that is not of God heareth not us. Hereby know we the spirit of truth, and the spirit of error. (1 John 4:1-6)

King's kid report: Victory 284-90

My personal experience:

Manufacturer's Handbook

God's answer: All scripture is given by inspiration of God, and is profitable for doctrine, for reproof, for correction, for instruction in righteousness. (2 Timothy 3:16)

Knowing this first, that no prophecy of the scripture is of any private interpretation. For the prophecy came not in old time by the will of man: but holy men of God spake as they were moved by the Holy Ghost. (2 Peter 1:20-21)

Heaven and earth shall pass away, but my words shall not pass away. (Matthew 24:35)

Thy word is truth. (John 17:17b)

King's kid report: Goo 17; King's Kid 25-26, 31; Winner 10, 15-16; Victory 83, 122-23, 136-39

My personal experience:

Mark 16/17-18, Victory 90-98
Marriage problems. See **Husband-Wife Haggles**
Martyr pills. See **Pity Parties**

Mediums

God's answer: There shall not be found among you anyone who makes his son or his daughter pass through the fire, one who uses divination, one who practices witchcraft, or one who interprets omens, or a sorcerer, or one who casts a spell, or a medium, or a spiritist, or one who calls up the dead. For whoever does these things is detestable to the Lord. (Deuteronomy 18:10-12a NAS)

I will set my face against anyone who consults mediums and wizards instead of me and I will cut that person off from his people. (Leviticus 20:6 TLB)

King's kid report: King's Kid 180-82; Winner 71-77

My personal experience:

Miracles

God's answer: For to one is given by the Spirit the word of wisdom . . . To another the working of miracles. (1 Corinthians 12:8a, 10a)

But as many as received him, to them gave he power to become the sons of God, even to them that believe on his name. (John 1:12)

Verily, verily, I say unto you, He that believeth on me, the works that I do shall he do also: and greater works than these shall he do; because I go unto my Father. (John 14:12)

Now you have every grace and blessing; every spiritual gift and power for doing his will are yours during this time of waiting for the return of our Lord Jesus Christ. (1 Corinthians 1:7 TLB)

Jesus said unto him, If thou canst believe, all things are possible to him that believeth. (Mark 9:23)

King's kid report: King's Kid 152-55, 189-95; Victory 235, 273, 307

My personal experience:

Mirror Principle, Victory 65-67

Missing Day

God's answer: And the sun stood still, and the moon stayed, until the people had avenged themselves upon their enemies. Is not this written in the book of Jasher? So the sun stood still in the midst of heaven, and hasted not to go down about a whole day. (Joshua 10:13)

And Isaiah the prophet cried unto the Lord: and he brought the shadow ten degrees backward, by which it had gone down in the dial of Ahaz. (2 Kings 20:11)

King's kid report: King's Kid 65-77

My personal experience:

Mohammedanism, King's Kid 19
Money. See **Tithing**
Moon Walk, King's Kid 65-66
Mortgage foreclosure. See **Property Problems**
Moses, Victory 37, 49, 108, 127, 169

Motor-mouthing. See **Blabbermouths; Grumbling**
Mount of Transfiguration, Victory 28
Mudball origins. See **Potter and the Clay**
Mudites, Victory 17
Narcotics. See names of particular narcotics, e.g., **Heroin;
LSD,** etc.
NASA, King's Kid 65, 71-72, 121

Negative Confession

God's answer: Death and life are in the power of the
tongue. (Proverbs 18:21a)

A wholesome tongue is a tree of life: but perverseness
therein is a breach in the spirit. (Proverbs 15:4)

Set a watch, O Lord, before my mouth; keep the door of
my lips. (Psalm 141:3)

King's kid report: Victory 69, 222-24

My personal experience:

Nervous Imbalance, King's Kid 173-77

New creation. See **Born Again, How to Be**

New Management

God's answer: Therefore if any man be in Christ, he is a new creature: old things are passed away; behold, all things are become new. And all things are of God, who hath reconciled us to himself by Jesus Christ, and hath given to us the ministry of reconciliation. (2 Corinthians 5:17-18)

But we have this treasure in earthen vessels, that the excellency of the power may be of God, and not of us. (2 Corinthians 4:7)

I am crucified with Christ: nevertheless I live; yet not I, but Christ liveth in me: and the life which I now live in the flesh I live by the faith of the Son of God, who loved me, and gave himself for me. (Galatians 2:20)

King's kid report: King's Kid 14; Winner xv, 13; Victory 218; Goo 89-90

My personal experience:

Nit-picking. See **Grumbling; Husband-Wife Haggles**
Noah, Goo 56-59

Obedience

God's answer: And Samuel said, Hath the Lord as great
delight in burnt offerings and sacrifices, as in obeying the
voice of the Lord? Behold, to obey is better than sacrifice,
and to hearken than the fat of rams. (1 Samuel 15:22)

Blessed rather are those who hear the word of God and
obey it. (Luke 11:28 NIV)

God blesses those who obey him; happy the man who puts
his trust in the Lord. (Proverbs 16:20 TLB)

And when we obey him, every path he guides us on is
fragrant with his lovingkindness and his truth. (Psalm
25:10 TLB)

But if you stay in me and obey my commands, you may ask
any request you like, and it will be granted! (John 15:7
TLB)

King's kid report: Victory 70-71, 153-55, 162-65

My personal experience:

Obstetrics, Heavenly, Victory 133, 260
Occult. See **Automatic Writing, Horoscopes, Mediums, Ouija Boards, Witchcraft**
Old Folks' Homes, Victory 227-30

Ouija Boards

God's answer: There shall not be found among you anyone who makes his son or his daughter pass through the fire, one who uses divination, one who practices witchcraft, or one who interprets omens, or a sorcerer, or one who casts a spell, or a medium, or a spiritist, or one who calls up the dead. For whoever does these things is detestable to the Lord. (Deuteronomy 18:10-12a NAS)

King's kid report: King's Kid 179; Winner 149, 183-84; Victory 296

My personal experience:

Overeating

God's answer: Bless the Lord, O my soul, and forget not all his benefits: Who satisfieth thy mouth with good things; so that thy youth is renewed like the eagle's. (Psalm 103:2, 5)

And seek not ye what ye shall eat, or what ye shall drink, neither be ye of doubtful mind. (Luke 12:29)

Therefore I say unto you, Take no thought for your life, what ye shall eat, or what ye shall drink; nor yet for your body, what ye shall put on. Is not the life more than meat, and the body than raiment? (Matthew 6:25)

King's kid report: Victory 77

My personal experience:

Ownership vs. Stewardship

God's answer: The earth is the Lord's, and the fulness thereof; the world, and they that dwell therein. (Psalm 24:1)

For of him, and through him, and to him, are all things: to whom be glory for ever. Amen. (Romans 11:36)

For what is a man profited, if he shall gain the whole world, and lose his own soul? (Matthew 16:26a)

Lay not up for yourselves treasures upon earth, where moth and rust doth corrupt, and where thieves break through and steal: But lay up for yourselves treasures in heaven, where neither moth nor rust doth corrupt, and where thieves do not break through nor steal: For where your treasure is, there will your heart be also. (Matthew 6:19-21)

And he said unto them, Take heed, and beware of covetousness: for a man's life consisteth not in the abundance of the things which he possesseth. (Luke 12:15)

King's kid report: King's Kid 149-55; Winner xvii-xix, 82-83, 165-66, 169-74; Victory 72-74, 78-81

My personal experience:

Pacifist, King's Kid 167-71
Pain, Winner 29-32

Paralysis of Analysis

God's answer: For if any be a hearer of the word, and not a doer, he is like unto a man beholding his natural face in a glass: For he beholdeth himself, and goeth his way, and straightway forgetteth what manner of man he was. But whoso looketh into the perfect law of liberty, and continueth therein, he being not a forgetful hearer, but a doer of the work, this man shall be blessed in his deed. (James 1:23-25)

But the natural man receiveth not the things of the Spirit of God: for they are foolishness unto him: neither can he know them, because they are spiritually discerned. (1 Corinthians 2:14)

Beware lest any man spoil you through philosophy and vain deceit, after the tradition of men, after the rudiments of the world, and not after Christ. (Colossians 2:8)

King's kid report: King's Kid xi

My personal experience:

Patience. See **Impatience**
Paul and Silas, Victory 306-7

Peace
   God's answer: Thou wilt keep him in perfect peace, whose mind is stayed on thee: because he trusteth in thee. (Isaiah 26:3)

   Peace I leave with you, my peace I give unto you: not as the world giveth, give I unto you. Let not your heart be troubled, neither let it be afraid. (John 14:27)

   And the very God of peace sanctify you wholly; and I pray God your whole spirit and soul and body be preserved blameless unto the coming of our Lord Jesus Christ. (1 Thessalonians 5:23)

   King's kid report: King's Kid 24; Goo 62-63; Victory 299-300

   My personal experience:

Philosophy

God's answer: Beware lest any man spoil you through philosophy and vain deceit, after the tradition of men, after the rudiments of the world, and not after Christ. (Colossians 2:8)

And again, The Lord knoweth the thoughts of the wise, that they are vain. Therefore let no man glory in men. For all things are yours. (1 Corinthians 3:20-21)

Wherefore lay apart all filthiness and superfluity of naughtiness, and receive with meekness the engrafted word, which is able to save your souls. But be ye doers of the word, and not hearers only, deceiving your own selves. (James 1:21-22)

King's kid report: King's Kid 167-71; Victory 18-23, 293-300

My personal experience:

Pity Parties

God's answer: Casting down imaginations, and every high thing that exalteth itself against the knowledge of God, and bringing into captivity every thought to the obedience of Christ. (2 Corinthians 10:5)

It is the thought-life that pollutes. For from within, out of men's hearts, come evil thoughts of lust, theft, murder, adultery, wanting what belongs to others, wickedness, deceit, lewdness, envy, slander, pride, and all other folly. All these vile things come from within; they are what pollute you and make you unfit for God. (Mark 7:20-23 TLB)

Let the words of my mouth, and the meditation of my heart, be acceptable in thy sight, O Lord, my strength, and my redeemer. (Psalm 19:14)

For as he thinketh in his heart, so is he. (Proverbs 23:7a)

King's kid report: King's Kid 72, 108, 142, 204; Winner 37, 99; Victory 73, 106, 160, 197, 305

My personal experience:

Plato, King's Kid 20

Poker. See **Gambling**

Poison

God's answer: And these signs shall follow them that believe . . . and if they drink any deadly thing, it shall not hurt them. (Mark 16:17-18)

King's kid report: King's Kid 111-12, 152-55; Victory 96

My personal experience:

Possessiveness. See **Ownership vs. Stewardship**

Potter and the Clay

God's answer: But now, O Lord, thou art our father; we are the clay, and thou our potter; and we all are the work of thy hand. (Isaiah 64:8)

O house of Israel, cannot I do with you as this potter? saith the Lord. Behold, as the clay is in the potter's hand, so are ye in mine hand, O house of Israel. (Jeremiah 18:6)

Hath not the potter power over the clay, of the same lump to make one vessel unto honour, and another unto dishonour? (Romans 9:21)

King's kid report: Victory 53-60

My personal experience:

133

Power Hookup, Winner 75-77

Power Shortage

God's answer: But you shall receive power, when the Holy Spirit has come upon you. (Acts 1:8a RSV)

John answered, saying unto them all, I indeed baptize you with water; but one mightier than I cometh, the latchet of whose shoes I am not worthy to unloose: he shall baptize you with the Holy Ghost and with fire. (Luke 3:16)

Behold, I give unto you power to tread on serpents and scorpions, and over all the power of the enemy: and nothing shall by any means hurt you. (Luke 10:19)

But as many as received him, to them gave he power to become the sons of God, even to them that believe on his name. (John 1:12)

That he would grant you, according to the riches of his glory, to be strengthened with might by his Spirit in the inner man. (Ephesians 3:16)

God is my strength and power: and he maketh my way perfect. (2 Samuel 22:33)

King's kid report: King's Kid 53-58; Winner 15-20; Victory 84-89, 250-52

My personal experience:

Praise in Adversity (see also **Sacrifice of Praise;** and specific adversities, e.g., **Arthritis, Firebombs, Heart Trouble, Highway Accidents, Lions,** etc.)

God's answer: I will bless the Lord at all times: his praise shall continually be in my mouth. (Psalm 34:1)

Whoso offereth praise glorifieth me: and to him that ordereth his conversation aright will I show the salvation of God. (Psalm 50:23)

But thou art holy, O thou that inhabitest the praises of Israel. (Psalm 22:3)

O praise the Lord, all ye nations: praise him, all ye people. For his merciful kindness is great toward us; and the truth of the Lord endureth for ever. Praise ye the Lord. (Psalm 117:1-2)

King's kid report: King's Kid 125-45, 207-13; Winner 39-47, 56-58, 85-93, 95-100, 116-20, 132-33, 169-74; Victory 44-46, 68-71, 184-87, 219-21

My personal experience:

Prayer, Answered

God's answer: And whatsoever we ask, we receive of him, because we keep his commandments, and do those things that are pleasing in his sight. (1 John 3:22)

And this is the confidence that we have in him, that, if we ask any thing according to his will, he heareth us: And if we know that he hear us, whatsoever we ask, we know that we have the petitions that we desired of him. (1 John 5:14-15)

Therefore I say unto you, What things soever ye desire, when ye pray, believe that ye receive them, and ye shall have them. And when ye stand praying, forgive, if ye have ought against any: that your Father also which is in heaven may forgive you your trespasses. (Mark 11:24-25)

Verily I say unto you, Whatsoever ye shall bind on earth shall be bound in heaven: and whatsoever ye shall loose on earth shall be loosed in heaven. (Matthew 18:18)

If ye abide in me, and my words abide in you, ye shall ask what ye will, and it shall be done unto you. (John 15:7)

Delight thyself also in the Lord; and he shall give thee the desires of thine heart. (Psalm 37:4)

But they that wait upon the Lord shall renew their strength; they shall mount up with wings as eagles; they shall run, and not be weary; and they shall walk, and not faint. (Isaiah 40:31)

But if any man be a worshipper of God, and doeth his will, him he heareth. (John 9:31)

King's kid report: Winner 105-6; Victory 70-71, 105-14

My personal experience:

Prayer in the Spirit (see also **Tongues**)

God's answer: Wherefore let him that speaketh in an unknown tongue pray that he may interpret. For if I pray in an unknown tongue, my spirit prayeth, but my understanding is unfruitful. What is it then? I will pray with the spirit, and I will pray with the understanding also: I will sing with the spirit, and I will sing with the understanding also. (1 Corinthians 14:13-15)

Praying always with all prayer and supplication in the Spirit, and watching thereunto with all perseverance and supplication for all saints. (Ephesians 6:18)

But ye, beloved, building up yourselves on your most holy faith, praying in the Holy Ghost. (Jude 20)

King's kid report: King's Kid 122

My personal experience:

Prayer, Intercessory

God's answer: Likewise the Spirit also helpeth our infirmities: for we know not what we should pray for as we ought: but the Spirit itself maketh intercession for us with groanings which cannot be uttered. (Romans 8:26)

I exhort therefore, that, first of all, supplications, prayers, intercessions, and giving of thanks, be made for all men. (1 Timothy 2:1)

Confess your faults one to another, and pray one for another, that ye may be healed. (James 5:16)

Praying always with all prayer and supplication in the Spirit, and watching thereunto with all perseverance and supplication for all saints. (Ephesians 6:18)

King's kid report: King's Kid 1-7, 79-85, 112-16, 121-22, 152-55; Winner 35, 86; Victory 147, 209, 243-44, 249, 252

My personal experience:

Prayer of Unbelief

God's answer: Therefore I say unto you, What things soever ye desire, when ye pray, believe that ye receive them, and ye shall have them. (Mark 11:24)

Beloved, I wish above all things that thou mayest prosper and be in health, even as thy soul prospereth. (3 John 2)

And all things, whatsoever ye shall ask in prayer, believing, ye shall receive. (Matthew 21:22)

King's kid report: King's Kid 184; Winner 30-31; Victory 252

My personal experience:

Prayer, Proxy

God's answer: And when Jesus was entered into Capernaum, there came unto him a centurion, beseeching him, And saying, Lord, my servant lieth at home sick of the palsy, grievously tormented. And Jesus saith unto him, I will come and heal him. The centurion answered and said, Lord, I am not worthy that thou shouldest come under my roof: but speak the word only, and my servant shall be healed. . . . And his servant was healed in the selfsame hour. (Matthew 8:5-8, 13b)

King's kid report: King's Kid 173-77; Winner 155-56

My personal experience:

Prayer Without Ceasing

God's answer: Pray without ceasing. (1 Thessalonians 5:17)

King's kid report: King's Kid 79-81; Winner 98-100, 159-67

My personal experience:

Preacher, Perfect, King's Kid 142-43

Preaching
God's answer: For the Holy Ghost shall teach you in the same hour what ye ought to say. (Luke 12:12)

Open thy mouth wide, and I will fill it. (Psalm 81:10b)

Faithful is he that calleth you, who also will do it. (1 Thessalonians 5:24)

King's kid report: Winner 135-41

My personal experience:

Pride

God's answer: Pride goeth before destruction, and an haughty spirit before a fall. (Proverbs 16:18)

But the meek shall inherit the earth; and shall delight themselves in the abundance of peace. (Psalm 37:11)

The pride of life is not of the Father, but is of the world. (1 John 2:16b)

Wherefore he saith, God resisteth the proud, but giveth grace unto the humble. (James 4:6)

Humble yourselves in the sight of the Lord, and he shall lift you up. (James 4:10)

That, according as it is written, He that glorieth, let him glory in the Lord. (1 Corinthians 1:31)

Thus saith the Lord, Let not the wise man glory in his wisdom, neither let the mighty man glory in his might, let not the rich man glory in his riches: But let him that glorieth glory in this, that he understandeth and knoweth me, that I am the Lord which exercise lovingkindness, judgment, and righteousness, in the earth: for in these things I delight, saith the Lord. (Jeremiah 9:23-24)

King's kid report: King's Kid 105; Winner xvi; Victory 77-78, 97,237-39, 274

My personal experience:

Prison. See **Bum Rap**

Programitis

God's answer: For they being ignorant of God's righteousness, and going about to establish their own righteousness, have not submitted themselves unto the righteousness of God. (Romans 10:3)

The Lord's blessing is our greatest wealth. All our work adds nothing to it! (Proverbs 10:22 TLB)

King's kid report: Victory 153, 215

My personal experience:

Promised Land, Goo 72-73; Victory 31-34

Property Problems
God's answer: Rejoice in the Lord alway: and again I say, Rejoice. (Philippians 4:4)

Fear ye not, stand still, and see the salvation of the Lord, which he will shew to you today. (Exodus 14:13)

But my God shall supply all your need according to his riches in glory by Christ Jesus. (Philippians 4:19)

King's kid report: Winner 107-12, 159-67

My personal experience:

Prophecy

God's answer: Follow after charity, and desire spiritual gifts, but rather that ye may prophesy. For he that speaketh in an unknown tongue speaketh not unto men, but unto God: for no man understandeth him; howbeit in the spirit he speaketh mysteries. But he that prophesieth speaketh unto men to edification, and exhortation, and comfort. He that speaketh in an unknown tongue edifieth himself; but he that prophesieth edifieth the church. I would that ye all spake with tongues, but rather that ye prophesied: for greater is he that prophesieth than he that speaketh with tongues, except he interpret, that the church may receive edifying. (1 Corinthians 14:1-5)

In the mouth of two or three witnesses shall every word be established. (2 Corinthians 13:1b)

But the natural man receiveth not the things of the Spirit of God: for they are foolishness unto him: neither can he know them, because they are spiritually discerned. (1 Corinthians 2:14)

Wherefore, brethren, covet to prophesy, and forbid not to speak with tongues. (1 Corinthians 14:39)

And though I have the gift of prophecy, and understand all mysteries, and all knowledge; and though I have all faith, so that I could remove mountains, and have not charity, I am nothing. (1 Corinthians 13:2)

Despise not prophesyings. (1 Thessalonians 5:20)

And the spirits of the prophets are subject to the prophets. (1 Corinthians 14:32)

King's kid report: King's Kid 65, 158, 192; Winner 109; Victory 253-58

My personal experience:

Proxy prayer. See **Prayer, Proxy**

Pruning

God's answer: I am the true vine, and my Father is the husbandman. Every branch in me that beareth not fruit he taketh away: and every branch that beareth fruit, he purgeth it, that it may bring forth more fruit. (John 15:1-2)

King's kid report: Victory 124-26, 131-35

My personal experience:

Psalm 23, Victory 151-61

Psychiatry

God's answer: Don't look to men for help; their greatest leaders fail. (Psalm 146:3 TLB)

With men it is impossible, but not with God: for with God all things are possible. (Mark 10:27)

Now ye are clean through the word which I have spoken unto you. (John 15:3)

And so, dear brothers, now we may walk right into the very Holy of Holies where God is, because of the blood of Jesus. This is the fresh, new, life-giving way which Christ has opened up for us by tearing the curtain—his human body—to let us into the holy presence of God. (Hebrews 10:19-20 TLB)

Therefore if any man be in Christ, he is a new creature: old things are passed away; behold, all things are become new. And all things are of God, who hath reconciled us to himself by Jesus Christ, and hath given to us the ministry of reconciliation. (2 Corinthians 5:17-18)

The heart is deceitful above all things, and desperately wicked: who can know it? (Jeremiah 17:9)

King's kid report: King's Kid 10, 21, 179-87; Goo 63; Winner 65-66; Victory 35-36

My personal experience:

Psychologist, King's Kid 184-87

Purse-Snatching
God's answer: Surely he shall deliver thee from the snare of the fowler, and from the noisome pestilence. He shall cover thee with his feathers, and under his wings shalt thou trust: his truth shall be thy shield and buckler. Thou shalt not be afraid for the terror by night; nor for the arrow that flieth by day; Nor for the pestilence that walketh in darkness; nor for the destruction that wasteth at noonday. (Psalm 91:3-6)

So shall my word be that goeth forth out of my mouth: it shall not return unto me void, but it shall accomplish that which I please, and it shall prosper in the thing whereto I sent it. (Isaiah 55:11)

King's kid report: Victory 19-20

My personal experience:

Quick Mud

God's answer: Save me, O God; for the waters are come in unto my soul. I sink in deep mire, where there is no standing. . . . Deliver me out of the mire, and let me not sink: let me be delivered from them that hate me, and out of the deep waters. (Psalm 69:1-2a, 14)

King's kid report: King's Kid 17-22

My personal experience:

Reacting vs. Responding

God's answer: As ye have therefore received Christ Jesus the Lord, so walk ye in him. (Colossians 2:6)

But now ye also put off all these: anger, wrath, malice, blasphemy, filthy communication out of your mouth. Lie not one to another, seeing that ye have put off the old man with his deeds; And have put on the new man, which is renewed in knowledge after the image of him that created him. (Colossians 3:8-10)

Ye have heard that it hath been said, An eye for an eye, and a tooth for a tooth: But I say unto you, That ye resist not evil: but whosoever shall smite thee on thy right cheek, turn to him the other also. And if any man will sue thee at the law, and take away thy coat, let him have thy cloak also. And whosoever shall compel thee to go a mile, go with him twain. Give to him that asketh thee, and from him that would borrow of thee turn not thou away. Ye have heard that it hath been said, Thou shalt love thy neighbour, and hate thine enemy. But I say unto you, Love your enemies, bless them that curse you, do good to them that hate you, and pray for them which despitefully use you, and persecute you; That ye may be the children of your Father which is in heaven: for he maketh his sun to rise on the evil and on the good, and sendeth rain on the just and on the unjust. For if ye love them which love you, what reward have ye? do not even the publicans the same? And if ye salute your brethren only, what do ye more than others? do not even the publicans so? Be ye therefore perfect, even as your Father which is in heaven is perfect. (Matthew 5:38-48)

King's kid report: Winner xvii, 173-74; Victory 74, 80, 185

My personal experience:

Rebellion

God's answer: Anyone willing to be corrected is on the pathway to life. Anyone refusing has lost his chance. (Proverbs 10:17 TLB)

My son, despise not thou the chastening of the Lord, nor faint when thou art rebuked of him: For whom the Lord loveth he chasteneth, and scourgeth every son whom he receiveth. If ye endure chastening, God dealeth with you as with sons; for what son is he whom the father chasteneth not? Now no chastening for the present seemeth to be joyous, but grievous: nevertheless afterward it yieldeth the peaceable fruit of righteousness unto them which are exercised thereby. (Hebrews 12:5b-7, 11)

For rebellion is as the sin of witchcraft. (1 Samuel 15:23a)

King's kid report: Goo 51-60; Victory 40-41, 158, 182, 282-83, 292

My personal experience:

Recipe For Healing

God's answer: And these signs shall follow them that believe . . . they shall lay hands on the sick, and they shall recover. (Mark 16:17a, 18b)

Verily, verily, I say unto you, He that believeth on me, the works that I do shall he do also; and greater works than these shall he do; because I go unto my Father. And whatsoever ye shall ask in my name, that will I do, that the Father may be glorified in the Son. (John 14:12-13)

King's kid report: Victory 99-103

My personal experience:

Reliance. See **Self-reliance**
Reliance on God's Word. See **Doers of The Word**

Reliance On Other People

God's answer: Don't look to men for help; their greatest leaders fail; for every man must die. His breathing stops, life ends, and in a moment all he planned for himself is ended. But happy is the man who has the God of Jacob as his helper, whose hope is in the Lord his God—the God who made both earth and heaven, the seas and everything in them. He is the God who keeps every promise. (Psalm 146:3-6 TLB)

Therefore let no man glory in men. For all things are yours. (1 Corinthians 3:21)

Be not ye called Rabbi: for one is your Master, even Christ; and all ye are brethren. And call no man your father upon the earth: for one is your Father, which is in heaven. Neither be ye called masters: for one is your Master, even Christ. (Matthew 23:8-10)

The Lord will perfect that which concerneth me. (Psalm 138:8a)

King's kid report: Victory 47-50

My personal experience:

157

Religion, Winner 154
Relinquishment. See **Surrender**
Renewed strength. See **Strength, Renewed**

Rental Car Shortage

God's answer: Delight thyself also in the Lord; and he shall give thee the desires of thine heart. Commit thy way unto the Lord; trust also in him; and he shall bring it to pass. (Psalm 37:4-5)

Don't worry about anything; instead, pray about everything; tell God your needs and don't forget to thank him for his answers. (Philippians 4:6 TLB)

He will always give you all you need from day to day if you will make the Kingdom of God your primary concern. (Luke 12:31 TLB)

King's kid report: Winner 121-25

My personal experience:

Resentment. See **Broken Relationships**
Reservations, non-existent. See **Hotel No-Vacancy Signs; Travel Snags**
Rest, Victory 33-37

Resurrection

God's answer: That if thou shalt confess with thy mouth the Lord Jesus, and shalt believe in thine heart that God hath raised him from the dead, thou shalt be saved. (Romans 10:9)

Therefore if any man be in Christ, he is a new creature: old things are passed away; behold, all things are become new. (2 Corinthians 5:17)

For God so loved the world, that he gave his only begotten Son, that whosoever believeth in him should not perish, but have everlasting life. (John 3:16)

Now if Christ be preached that he rose from the dead, how say some among you that there is no resurrection of the dead? But if there be no resurrection of the dead, then is Christ not risen: And if Christ be not risen, then is our preaching vain, and your faith is also vain. Yea, and we are found false witnesses of God; because we have testified of God that he raised up Christ: whom he raised not up, if so be that the dead rise not. For if the dead rise not, then is not Christ raised: And if Christ be not raised, your faith is vain; ye are yet in your sins. Then they also which are fallen asleep in Christ are perished. If in this life only we have hope in Christ, we are of all men most miserable. But now is Christ risen from the dead, and become the firstfruits of them that slept. (1 Corinthians 15:12-20)

King's kid report: Goo 67-69

My personal experience:

Retirement

God's answer: And I will restore to you the years that the locust hath eaten, the cankerworm, and the caterpiller, and the palmerworm, my great army which I sent among you. And ye shall eat in plenty, and be satisfied, and praise the name of the Lord your God, that hath dealt wondrously with you: and my people shall never be ashamed. (Joel 2:25-26)

There remaineth therefore a rest to the people of God. For he that is entered into his rest, he also hath ceased from his own works, as God did from his. (Hebrews 4:9-10)

King's kid report: Victory 36-37

My personal experience:

161

Rights. See **Self-Rights**
Rinehart, Ed, Victory 205-11
Rioters. See **Firebombs**

Roadblocks to Wholeness (see also **Impatience; Unbelief; Unforgiveness**)
God's answer: Therefore I say unto you, What things soever ye desire, when ye pray, believe that ye receive them, and ye shall have them. And when ye stand praying, forgive, if ye have ought against any: that your Father also which is in heaven may forgive you your trespasses. (Mark 11:24-25)

Wait on the Lord: be of good courage, and he shall strengthen thine heart: wait, I say, on the Lord. (Psalm 27:14)

King's kid report: King's Kid 107, 111, 199; Victory, 88, 192, 195

My personal experience:

162

Rockets, Falling, King's Kid 121-22

Sacrifice of Praise
God's answer: By him therefore let us offer the sacrifice of praise to God continually, that is, the fruit of our lips giving thanks to his name. (Hebrews 13:15)

But true praise is a worthy sacrifice; this really honors me. Those who walk my paths will receive salvation from the Lord. (Psalm 50:23 TLB)

King's kid report: King's Kid 118, 211; Victory 186-87

My personal experience:

Satan (see also **Demons**)

God's answer: For we wrestle not against flesh and blood, but against principalities, against powers, against the rulers of the darkness of this world, against spiritual wickedness in high places. (Ephesians 6:12)

Be sober, be vigilant; because your adversary the devil, as a roaring lion, walketh about, seeking whom he may devour. (1 Peter 5:8)

Submit yourselves therefore to God. Resist the devil, and he will flee from you. (James 4:7)

Kings kid report: King's Kid 57; Goo 53; Winner 183-86; Victory 95

My personal experience:

Scoffers (see also **Unbelief**)

God's answer: Knowing this first, that there shall come in the last days scoffers, walking after their own lusts. (2 Peter 3:3)

Dear friends, remember what the apostles of our Lord Jesus Christ told you, that in the last times there would come these scoffers whose whole purpose in life is to enjoy themselves in every evil way imaginable. (Jude 17 TLB)

King's kid report: King's Kid 74, 84-85

My personal experience:

Seances. See **Mediums**
Second Best, Victory 134-35, 299
Secretaries, God's, Victory 239

Self-Awareness
God's answer: For if a man think himself to be something,
when he is nothing, he deceiveth himself. (Galatians 6:3)

Look not every man on his own things, but every man also
on the things of others. (Philippians 2:4)

Let him who boasts, boast of the Lord. For it is not the
man who commends himself that is accepted, but the man
whom the Lord commends. (2 Corinthians 10:17-18 RSV)

This I say therefore, and testify in the Lord, that ye
henceforth walk not as other Gentiles walk, in the vanity
of their mind. (Ephesians 4:17)

King's kid report: Victory 297

My personal experience:

Self-Reliance (see also **Educated Idiots and the Educated Idiot Box**)

God's answer: So what about these wise men, these scholars, these brilliant debaters of this world's great affairs? God has made them all look foolish, and shown their wisdom to be useless nonsense. For God in his wisdom saw to it that the world would never find God through human brilliance, and then he stepped in and saved all those who believed his message, which the world calls foolish and silly. (1 Corinthians 1:20-21 TLB)

Verily I say unto you, Except ye be converted, and become as little children, ye shall not enter into the kingdom of heaven. (Matthew 18:3)

Not that we are sufficient of ourselves to think any thing as of ourselves; but our sufficiency is of God. (2 Corinthians 3:5)

I can do all things through Christ which strengtheneth me. (Philippians 4:13)

Trust in the Lord with all thine heart; and lean not unto thine own understanding. (Proverbs 3:5)

King's kid report: King's Kid xi-xii; Winner 166-67; Victory 34-35, 41-42, 75-76, 168-72, 216-21

My personal experience:

Self-Rights

God's answer: For none of us liveth to himself, and no man dieth to himself. For whether we live, we live unto the Lord; and whether we die, we die unto the Lord: whether we live therefore, or die, we are the Lord's. (Romans 14:7-8)

But so shall it not be among you: but whosoever will be great among you, shall be your minister: And whosoever of you will be the chiefest, shall be servant of all. (Mark 10:43-44)

Verily, verily, I say unto you, Except a corn of wheat fall into the ground and die, it abideth alone: but if it die, it bringeth forth much fruit. He that loveth his life shall lose it; and he that hateth his life in this world shall keep it unto life eternal. (John 12:24-25)

Blessed are the poor in spirit: for theirs is the kingdom of heaven. (Matthew 5:3)

I am crucified with Christ: nevertheless I live; yet not I, but Christ liveth in me: and the life which I now live in the flesh I live by the faith of the Son of God, who loved me, and gave himself for me. (Galatians 2:20)

King's kid report: Winner xviii-xix; Victory 73, 77-81, 298

My personal experience:

Sheep and the Shepherd, Victory 151-61
Shoemaker, Sam, Victory 206
Sick heads. See **Blown Minds**
Sickness. See name of particular ailment; e.g., **Cancer,**
Heart Trouble, etc.

Singlemindedness

God's answer: No servant can serve two masters: for
either he will hate the one, and love the other; or else he
will hold to the one, and despise the other. Ye cannot
serve God and mammon. (Luke 16:13)

Ye cannot drink the cup of the Lord, and the cup of devils:
ye cannot be partakers of the Lord's table, and of the table
of devils. (1 Corinthians 10:21)

A double minded man is unstable in all his ways. (James
1:8)

Draw nigh to God, and he will draw nigh to you. Cleanse
your hands, ye sinners; and purify your hearts, ye double
minded. (James 4:8)

King's kid report: Victory 202

My personal experience:

Sluefoot. See **Satan**

Smoking

God's answer: For ye are bought with a price: therefore glorify God in your body, and in your spirit, which are God's. (1 Corinthians 6:20)

I beseech you therefore, brethren, by the mercies of God, that ye present your bodies a living sacrifice, holy, acceptable unto God, which is your reasonable service. (Romans 12:1)

Know ye not that ye are the temple of God, and that the Spirit of God dwelleth in you? If any man defile the temple of God, him shall God destroy: for the temple of God is holy, which temple ye are. (1 Corinthians 3:16-17)

For a man is a slave to whatever has mastered him. (2 Peter 2:19b NIV)

King's kid report: King's Kid 93-97; Winner 179-83

My personal experience:

Snake (as Satan), Goo 53
Snakes, Victory 96
Snowed-in highways. See **Blizzards**
Solomon, Victory 233, 248
Soul vs. Spirit, Victory 34-35
Sound Equipment, Stolen, Winner 169-74
Sower, the, Victory 145-46
Space Science, King's Kid 65-77
Spiritual drought. See **Fruit Bearing**

Spiritual Experience

God's answer: For if any be a hearer of the word, and not a doer, he is like unto a man beholding his natural face in a glass: For he beholdeth himself, and goeth his way, and straightway forgetteth what manner of man he was. But whoso looketh into the perfect law of liberty, and continueth therein, he being not a forgetful hearer, but a doer of the work, this man shall be blessed in his deed. (James 1:23-25)

Verily I say unto you, Inasmuch as ye have done it unto one of the least of these my brethren, ye have done it unto me. (Matthew 25:40b)

King's kid report: Victory 11-17

My personal experience:

Strength, Renewed

God's answer: They that wait upon the Lord shall renew their strength; they shall mount up with wings as eagles; they shall run, and not be weary; they shall walk, and not faint. (Isaiah 40:31)

He leadeth me beside the still waters. He restoreth my soul. (Psalm 23:2b, 3a)

A new heart also will I give you, and a new spirit will I put within you: and I will take away the stony heart out of your flesh, and I will give you an heart of flesh. (Ezekiel 36:26)

Therefore if any man be in Christ, he is a new creature: old things are passed away; behold, all things are become new. (2 Corinthians 5:17)

King's kid report: Victory 213-15

My personal experience:

Stress (see also **Anxiety**)

God's answer: Commit thy works unto the Lord, and thy thoughts shall be established. (Proverbs 16:3)

Thou wilt keep him in perfect peace, whose mind is stayed on thee: because he trusteth in thee. (Isaiah 26:3)

Peace I leave with you, my peace I give unto you: not as the world giveth, give I unto you. Let not your heart be troubled, neither let it be afraid. (John 14:27)

These things I have spoken unto you, that in me ye might have peace. In the world ye shall have tribulation: but be of good cheer; I have overcome the world. (John 16:33)

That he would grant you, according to the riches of his glory, to be strengthened with might by his Spirit in the inner man. (Ephesians 3:16)

Faithful is he that calleth you, who also will do it. (1 Thessalonians 5:24)

King's kid report: Goo 62-63, 76-77; Victory 83-89, 299-300

My personal experience:

Stumbling Block

God's answer: Let us not therefore judge one another any more: but judge this rather, that no man put a stumbling block or an occasion to fall in his brother's way. (Romans 14:13)

It is good neither to eat flesh, nor to drink wine, nor any thing whereby thy brother stumbleth, or is offended, or is made weak. (Romans 14:21)

King's kid report: Victory 298

My personal experience:

Submission. See **Husband-Wife Haggles; Rebellion; Surrender**

Success, King's Kid 9-12; Victory 76

Suicide

God's answer: The thief cometh not, but for to steal, and to kill, and to destroy: I am come that they might have life, and that they might have it more abundantly. (John 10:10)

Come unto me, all ye that labour and are heavy laden, and I will give you rest. Take my yoke upon you, and learn of me; for I am meek and lowly in heart: and ye shall find rest unto your souls. For my yoke is easy, and my burden is light. (Matthew 11:28-30)

Let him have all your worries and cares, for he is always thinking about you and watching everything that concerns you. (1 Peter 5:7 TLB)

Draw nigh to God and he will draw nigh to you. (James 4:8a)

King's kid report: King's Kid 11-13, 152-55; Winner 44-45; Victory 250-52

My personal experience:

Supernatural

God's answer: Even the mystery which hath been hid from ages and from generations, but now is made manifest to his saints: To whom God would make known what is the riches of the glory of this mystery among the Gentiles; which is Christ in you, the hope of glory. (Colossians 1:26-28)

But the natural man receiveth not the things of the Spirit of God: for they are foolishness unto him: neither can he know them, because they are spiritually discerned. (1 Corinthians 2:14)

But to which of the angels said he at any time, Sit on my right hand, until I make thine enemies thy footstool? Are they not all ministering spirits, sent forth to minister for them who shall be heirs of salvation? (Hebrews 1:13-14)

King's kid report: Victory 86-89, 180

My personal experience:

Surrender (see also **Binding and Loosing; Ownership vs. Stewardship; Self-Reliance; Self-Rights**)

God's answer: I beseech you therefore, brethren, by the mercies of God, that ye present your bodies a living sacrifice, holy, acceptable unto God, which is your reasonable service. (Romans 12:1)

Then said Jesus unto his disciples, If any man will come after me, let him deny himself, and take up his cross and follow me. For whosoever will save his life shall lose it: and whosoever will lose his life for my sake shall find it. (Matthew 16:24-25)

And what agreement hath the temple of God with idols? for ye are the temple of the living God; as God hath said, I will dwell in them, and walk in them; and I will be their God, and they shall be my people. (2 Corinthians 6:16)

But we have this treasure in earthen vessels, that the excellency of the power may be of God, and not of us. (2 Corinthians 4:7)

King's kid report: Winner 13-14; Victory 53-60

My personal experience:

Sword, Two-Edged, Victory 37-38
Taming the tongue. See **Tongue Trouble**

Technical Difficulties

God's answer: Trust in the Lord with all thine heart; and lean not unto thine own understanding. In all thy ways acknowledge him, and he shall direct thy paths. (Proverbs 3:5-6)

And those whose faith has made them good in God's sight must live by faith, trusting him in everything. (Hebrews 10:38 TLB)

Commit thy works unto the Lord, and thy thoughts shall be established. (Proverbs 16:3)

King's kid report: King's Kid 157-65; Winner 32-37, 49-53

My personal experience:

Teeth (see also **Tooth Trouble**), Victory 22
Television. See **Boob-Tube-Itis**

Testimony

God's answer: And they overcame him by the blood of the Lamb, and by the word of their testimony. (Revelation 12:11)

Quietly trust yourself to Christ your Lord and if anybody asks why you believe as you do, be ready to tell him, and do it in a gentle and respectful way. (1 Peter 3:15 TLB)

King's kid report: King's Kid 57-63, 130-33; Winner 75-77, 186-87

My personal experience:

Thermodynamics, Goo 13-15

Think tanks. See **Ignorance**

Thorn in the Flesh

God's answer: And lest I should be exalted above measure
through the abundance of the revelations, there was given
to me a thorn in the flesh, the messenger of Satan to buffet
me, lest I should be exalted above measure. For this thing
I besought the Lord thrice, that it might depart from me.
And he said unto me, My grace is sufficient for thee: for
my strength is made perfect in weakness. (2 Corinthians
12:7-9a)

King's kid report: Victory 43-44

My personal experience:

Time That Marches On, Winner 85-93

Tithing

God's answer: Give, and it shall be given unto you; good measure, pressed down, and shaken together, and running over, shall men give into your bosom. For with the same measure that ye mete withal it shall be measured to you again. (Luke 6:38)

Bring ye all the tithes into the storehouse, that there may be meat in mine house, and prove me now herewith, saith the Lord of hosts, if I will not open you the windows of heaven, and pour you out a blessing, that there shall not be room enough to receive it. (Malachi 3:10)

King's kid report: King's Kid 31-37; Victory 79

My personal experience:

Tongue Trouble (see also **Gossip; Negative Confession**)

God's answer: So also the tongue is a small thing, but what enormous damage it can do. A great forest can be set on fire by one tiny spark. And the tongue is a flame of fire. It is full of wickedness, and poisons every part of the body. And the tongue is set on fire by hell itself, and can turn our whole lives into a blazing flame of destruction and disaster. (James 3:5-6 TLB)

Set a watch, O Lord, before my mouth; keep the door of my lips. (Psalm 141:3)

But as he which hath called you is holy, so be ye holy in all manner of conversation. (1 Peter 1:15)

King's kid report: Victory 68-74, 241-42

My personal experience:

Tongues (see also **Prayer in the Spirit**)

God's answer: And these signs shall follow them that believe . . . they shall speak with new tongues. (Mark 16:17)

And they were all filled with the Holy Ghost, and began to speak with other tongues, as the Spirit gave them utterance. (Acts 2:4)

He that speaketh in an unknown tongue edifieth himself. (1 Corinthians 14:4a)

Likewise the Spirit also helpeth our infirmities: for we know not what we should pray for as we ought: but the Spirit itself maketh intercession for us with groanings which cannot be uttered. (Romans 8:26)

Wherefore, brethren, covet to prophesy, and forbid not to speak with tongues. (1 Corinthians 14:39)

King's kid report: King's Kid 79-87; Victory 95-96, 235, 240-49

My personal experience:

Tooth Trouble

God's answer: Be careful for nothing; but in everything by prayer and supplication with thanksgiving let your requests be made known unto God. (Philippians 4:6)

I will bless the Lord at all times: his praise shall continually be in my mouth. (Psalm 34:1)

King's kid report: Victory 110-11

My personal experience:

Tornadoes

God's answer: The Lord is nigh unto all them that call upon him, to all that call upon him in truth. He will fulfil the desire of them that fear him: he also will hear their cry, and will save them. (Psalm 145:18-19)

And Jesus looking upon them saith, With men it is impossible, but not with God: for with God all things are possible. (Mark 10:27)

King's kid report: King's Kid 116-17

My personal experience:

Traffic

God's answer: Many are the afflictions of the righteous: but the Lord delivereth him out of them all. (Psalm 34:19)

Thou wilt keep him in perfect peace, whose mind is stayed on thee: because he trusteth in thee. (Isaiah 26:3)

Have no anxiety about anything, but in everything by prayer and supplication with thanksgiving let your requests be made known to God. And the peace of God, which passes all understanding, will keep your hearts and your minds in Christ Jesus. (Philippians 4:6-7 RSV)

I will praise the Lord no matter what happens. (Psalm 34:1a TLB)

King's kid report: King's Kid 89-92; Winner 85-93

My personal experience:

Transcendental Meditation

God's answer: Now the Spirit speaketh expressly, that in the latter times some shall depart from the faith, giving heed to seducing spirits, and doctrines of devils. (1 Timothy 4:1)

That he would grant you, according to the riches of his glory, to be strengthened with might by his Spirit in the inner man; That Christ may dwell in your hearts by faith; that ye, being rooted and grounded in love, May be able to comprehend with all saints what is the breadth, and length, and depth, and height; And to know the love of Christ, which passeth knowledge, that ye might be filled with all the fulness of God. (Ephesians 3:16-19)

King's kid report: Winner 183; Victory 293-96

My personal experience:

Travel Agents, Winner 151-57

Travel Snags (see also **Air Travel Problems; Blizzards; Car Trouble; Fog; Fouled-Up Flight Plans; Highway Accidents; Hotel No-Vacancy Signs; Language Barrier; Rental Car Shortage; Traffic**)
God's answer: Not that I speak in respect of want: for I have learned, in whatsoever state I am, therewith to be content. (Philippians 4:11)

But my God shall supply all your need according to his riches in glory by Christ Jesus. (Philippians 4:19)

Rejoice in the Lord alway: and again I say, Rejoice. (Philippians 4:4)

And we know that all things work together for good to them that love God, to them who are the called according to his purpose. (Romans 8:28)

Rejoice evermore. Pray without ceasing. In every thing give thanks: for this is the will of God in Christ Jesus concerning you. (1 Thessalonians 5:16-18)

King's kid report: King's Kid 206-9; Winner 113-20; Victory 118-20

My personal experience:

Trouble (see also names of specific troubles, e.g., **Arthritis; Back Trouble; Car Trouble; Property Problems; Tongue Trouble; Tooth Trouble,** etc.)

God's answer: Though I walk in the midst of trouble, thou wilt revive me: thou shalt stretch forth thine hand against the wrath of mine enemies, and thy right hand shall save me. (Psalm 138:7)

And call upon me in the day of trouble: I will deliver thee, and thou shalt glorify me. (Psalm 50:15)

Blessed be God, even the Father of our Lord Jesus Christ, the Father of mercies, and the God of all comfort; Who comforteth us in all our tribulation, that we may be able to comfort them which are in any trouble, by the comfort wherewith we ourselves are comforted of God. (2 Corinthians 1:3-4)

And not only so, but we glory in tribulations also: knowing that tribulation worketh patience; and patience, experience; and experience, hope. (Romans 5:3-4)

In the world ye shall have tribulation: but be of good cheer; I have overcome the world. (John 16:33b)

King's kid report: King's Kid 112-23; Winner 108; Victory 44-45, 187, 189-91

My personal experience:

Trust (see also **Doers of the Word**)

God's answer: Blessed is that man that maketh the Lord his trust, and respecteth not the proud, nor such as turn aside to lies. (Psalm 40:4)

The man who finds life will find it through trusting God. (Galatians 3:11b TLB)

Commit thy way unto the Lord; trust also in him; and he shall bring it to pass. (Psalm 37:5)

Trust ye in the Lord for ever: for in the Lord Jehovah is everlasting strength. (Isaiah 26:4)

For the Lord says, "Because he loves me, I will rescue him; I will make him great because he trusts in my name. When he calls on me I will answer; I will be with him in trouble, and rescue him and honor him. I will satisfy him with a full life and give him my salvation." (Psalm 91:14-16 TLB)

The fear of man bringeth a snare: but whoso putteth his trust in the Lord shall be safe. (Proverbs 29:25)

As for God, his way is perfect; the word of the Lord is tried: he is a buckler to all them that trust in him. (2 Samuel 22:31)

King's kid report: Victory 112, 189-91

My personal experience:

Twisted vision (TV). See **Boob-Tube-Itis**

Two (Better Than One)
God's answer: Two are better than one; because they have a good reward for their labour. (Ecclesiastes 4:9)

Again I say unto you, That if two of you shall agree on earth as touching any thing that they shall ask, it shall be done for them of my Father which is in heaven. (Matthew 18:19)

King's kid report: Victory 118-20, 176-77

My personal experience:

Tyson, Tommy, Victory 118-20

Ulcers

God's answer: Bless the Lord, O my soul: and all that is within me, bless his holy name. Bless the Lord, O my soul, and forget not all his benefits: Who forgiveth all thine iniquities; who healeth all thy diseases. (Psalm 103:1-3)

Verily I say unto you, Whatsoever ye shall bind on earth shall be bound in heaven: and whatsoever ye shall loose on earth shall be loosed in heaven. (Matthew 18:18)

If the Son therefore shall make you free, ye shall be free indeed. (John 8:36)

King's kid report: Victory 72

My personal experience:

Unbelief

God's answer: Take heed, brethren, lest there be in any of you an evil heart of unbelief, in departing from the living God . . . For we which have believed do enter into rest, as he said . . . And they to whom it was first preached entered not in because of unbelief. (Hebrews 3:12; 4:3a, 6b)

But the natural man receiveth not the things of the Spirit of God: for they are foolishness unto him: neither can he know them, because they are spiritually discerned. But he that is spiritual judgeth all things, yet he himself is judged of no man. For who hath known the mind of the Lord, that he may instruct him? But we have the mind of Christ. (1 Corinthians 2:14-16)

Unto the pure all things are pure: but unto them that are defiled and unbelieving is nothing pure; but even their mind and conscience is defiled. (Titus 1:15)

But the fearful, and unbelieving, and the abominable, and murderers and whoremongers, and sorcerers, and idolaters, and all liars, shall have their part in the lake which burneth with fire and brimstone: which is the second death. (Revelation 21:8)

King's kid report: King's Kid 167-71; Goo 72-75; Victory 31-39, 86-89, 113

My personal experience:

Unemployment

God's answer: Therefore take no thought, saying, What shall we eat? or, What shall we drink? or, Wherewithal shall we be clothed? (For after all these things do the Gentiles seek:) for your heavenly Father knoweth that ye have need of all these things. But seek ye first the kingdom of God, and his righteousness; and all these things shall be added unto you. (Matthew 6:31-33)

But my God shall supply all you need according to his riches in glory by Christ Jesus. (Philippians 4:19)

King's kid report: Victory 216-21

My personal experience:

Unforgiveness (see also **Broken Relationships**)
God's answer: Then came Peter to him and said, Lord, how oft shall my brother sin against me, and I forgive him? till seven times? Jesus saith unto him, I say not unto thee, Until seven times: but Until seventy times seven. (Matthew 18:21-22)

And when ye stand praying, forgive, if ye have ought against any: that your Father also which is in heaven may forgive you your trespasses. But if ye do not forgive, neither will your Father which is in heaven forgive your trespasses. (Mark 11:25-26)

King's kid report: King's Kid 199-204; Goo 75-78; Victory 192-204

My personal experience:

Unity

God's answer: This people draweth nigh unto me with their mouth, and honoreth me with their lips; but their heart is far from me. But in vain they do worship me, teaching for doctrines the commandments of men. (Matthew 15:8-9)

King's kid report: Victory 295

My personal experience:

Universalism

God's answer: Be not carried about with divers and strange doctrines. (Hebrews 13:9a)

Beware of false prophets, which come to you in sheep's clothing, but inwardly they are ravening wolves. Ye shall know them by their fruits. (Matthew 7:15-16a)

King's kid report: Victory 276-80, 294

My personal experience:

Unworthiness

God's answer: For all have sinned, and come short of the glory of God. (Romans 3:23)

Ye have not chosen me, but I have chosen you, and ordained you, that ye should go and bring forth fruit, and that your fruit should remain. (John 15:16a)

According as he hath chosen us in him before the foundation of the world, that we should be holy and without blame before him in love. (Ephesians 1:4)

Behold, what manner of love the Father hath bestowed upon us, that we should be called the sons of God. (1 John 3:1a)

But of him are ye in Christ Jesus, who of God is made unto us wisdom, and righteousness, and sanctification, and redemption. (1 Corinthians 1:30)

Come now, and let us reason together, saith the Lord: though your sins be as scarlet, they shall be as white as snow; though they be red like crimson, they shall be as wool. (Isaiah 1:18)

King's kid report: Goo 84-86; Winner 185-86; Victory 167-72, 275

My personal experience:

Waiting on the Lord
God's answer: They that wait upon the Lord shall renew their strength; they shall mount up with wings as eagles; they shall run, and not be weary; and they shall walk, and not faint. (Isaiah 40:31)

Wait on the Lord: be of good courage, and he shall strengthen thine heart: wait, I say, on the Lord. (Psalm 27:14)

King's kid report: Victory 213-15

My personal experience:

Warfare, Spiritual. See **Demons; Satan**

Weakness (see also **Strength, Renewed**)
God's answer: I am crucified with Christ: nevertheless I live; yet not I, but Christ liveth in me. (Galatians 2:20a)
But we have this treasure in earthen vessels, that the excellency of the power may be of God, and not of us. (2 Corinthians 4:7)
The Lord is the strength of my life. (Psalm 27: 1b)

My grace is sufficient for thee: for my strength is made perfect in weakness. Most gladly therefore will I rather glory in my infirmities, that the power of Christ may rest upon me. Therefore I take pleasure in infirmities, in reproaches, in necessities, in persecutions, in distresses for Christ's sake: for when I am weak, then am I strong. (2 Corinthians 12:9-10)

That he would grant you, according to the riches of his glory, to be strengthened with might by his Spirit in the inner man. (Ephesians 3:16)
He gives power to the tired and worn out, and strength to the weak. (Isaiah 40:29 TLB)

King's kid report: Winner xiv-xv, 193-94; Victory 42-46, 75-81

My personal experience:

Weights, Victory 75
Wholeness. See **Healing; Roadblocks to Wholeness**
Will of God. See **Doing God's Will**
Willpower. See **Drinking Too Much; Smoking**
Wisdom. See **Word of Wisdom**

Witchcraft

God's answer: Regard not them that have familiar spirits, neither seek after wizards, to be defiled by them. (Leviticus 19:31)

Idolatry, witchcraft, hatred, variance, emulations, wrath, strife, seditions, heresies, Envyings, murders, drunkenness, revellings, and such like: of the which I tell you before, as I have also told you in time past, that they which do such things shall not inherit the kingdom of God. (Galatians 5:20-21)

King's kid report: Winner 183, 188; Victory 298

My personal experience:

Witnessing

God's answer: But ye shall receive power, after that the Holy Ghost is come upon you: and ye shall be witnesses unto me both in Jerusalem and in all Judea, and in Samaria, and unto the uttermost part of the earth. (Acts 1:8)

But sanctify the Lord God in your hearts: and be ready always to give an answer to every man that asketh you a reason of the hope that is in you with meekness and fear. (1 Peter 3:15)

No man can come to me, except the Father which hath sent me draw him. (John 6:44a)

And I, if I be lifted up from the earth, will draw all men unto me. (John 12:32)

Behold, I send you forth as sheep in the midst of wolves: be ye therefore wise as serpents, and harmless as doves. (Matthew 10:16)

And the servant of the Lord must not strive; but be gentle unto all men, apt to teach, patient. (2 Timothy 2:24)

For the Holy Ghost shall teach you in the same hour what

ye ought to say. (Luke 12:12)

King's kid report: King's Kid 45-48, 53-63, 65, 70; Goo 83-84; Winner 21-26; Victory 140-48

My personal experience:

Wives. See **Husband-Wife Haggles**
Word of God (see also **Doers of the Word; Manufacturer's Handbook**), Victory 34

Word of Knowledge

God's answer: But the person who truly loves God is the one who is open to God's knowledge. (1 Corinthians 8:3 TLB)

For God giveth to a man that is good in his sight wisdom, and knowledge, and joy. (Ecclesiastes 2:26a)

. . . to another the word of knowledge by the same Spirit. (1 Corinthians 12:8b)

Now we have received, not the spirit of the world, but the spirit which is of God; that we might know the things that are freely given to us of God. (1 Corinthians 2:12)

King's kid report: King's Kid 1-4, 107-11, 167-71, 189-95; Winner 117-19, 129-32, 178-79; Victory 234, 266-68

My personal experience:

Word of Wisdom

God's answer: For to one is given by the Spirit the word of wisdom. (1 Corinthians 12:8a)

If any of you lack wisdom, let him ask of God, that giveth to all men liberally, and upbraideth not; and it shall be given him. (James 1:5)

For the Lord giveth wisdom: out of his mouth cometh knowledge and understanding. (Proverbs 2:6)

But if ye have bitter envying and strife in your hearts, glory not, and lie not against the truth. This wisdom descendeth not from above, but is earthly, sensual, devilish. For where envying and strife is, there is confusion and every evil work. But the wisdom that is from above is first pure, then peaceable, gentle, and easy to be intreated, full of mercy and good fruits, without partiality, and without hypocrisy. (James 3:14-17)

King's kid report: King's Kid 157-59, 191, 203; Winner xv; Victory 231-34, 278

My personal experience:

Worry. See **Anxiety**
Yoga, King's Kid 20; Victory 296
Zoroaster, King's Kid 21

For free information on how to receive
the international magazine

LOGOS JOURNAL

also Book Catalog

Write: Information - LOGOS JOURNAL CATALOG
Box 191
Plainfield, NJ 07061